ENTERPRISE ACT 2002

EXPLANATORY NOTES

INTRODUCTION

1. These explanatory notes relate to the Enterprise Act 2002 which received Royal Assent on 7 November 2002. They have been prepared by the Department of Trade and Industry (DTI) in order to assist the reader in understanding the Act. They do not form part of the Act and have not been endorsed by Parliament.

2. The notes need to be read in conjunction with the Act. They are not, and are not meant to be, a comprehensive description of the Act. So where a section or part of a section does not seem to require any explanation or comment, none is given.

OVERVIEW OF THE ACT

3. The Act is divided into eleven parts and has 281 sections and 26 Schedules.

4. Part 1: establishes the Office of Fair Trading (OFT), sets out its general functions, and provides for arrangements for making super-complaints to the OFT.

5. Part 2: establishes and makes provisions for proceedings before the Competition Appeal Tribunal (CAT).

6. Part 3: provides for a new merger regime, covering the definition of a qualifying merger, the duty of the OFT to make references to the Competition Commission (CC); how references are determined; the procedures that relate to certain public interest cases and other special cases; powers of enforcement; undertakings and orders; and various supplementary matters, such as information and publicity requirements and powers to require information.

7. Part 4: makes provision for new market investigations arrangements. It sets out the power of the OFT and the Secretary of State to make references to the CC, and how the CC should report on the references. It provides for particular arrangements to apply in public interest cases, and also covers powers of enforcement and various

supplementary matters.

8.   Part 5: deals with the CC, and provides for its rules of procedure.

9.   Part 6: deals with the creation of a cartel offence.

10.   Part 7: deals with a number of miscellaneous competition provisions, including powers to disqualify directors who engage in serious competition breaches.

11.   Part 8: deals with new procedures for enforcing certain consumer legislation, and miscellaneous related matters.

12.   Part 9: provides for rules to govern the disclosure of specified information held by a public authority, setting out the circumstances in which the information may be disclosed, and various related matters.

13.   Part 10: changes insolvency law by providing for a new regime for company administration and restricting the future use of administrative receivership; abolishing Crown preference; establishing a new regime for the insolvency of individuals; and making changes to the operation of the Insolvency Services Account.

14.   Part 11: contains a number of supplementary provisions, such as commencement, short title and territorial extent.

SUMMARY

15.   The Act implements a pledge in the Government's 2001 election manifesto to give more independence to the competition authorities, to reform the bankruptcy laws and to tackle trading practices that harm consumers. The White Paper *'Productivity in the UK: Enterprise and the Productivity Challenge'* (available at http://www.hmt.gov.uk/mediastore/otherfiles/26.pdf), published in June 2001, set out the Government's intention to focus on enterprise and productivity as the cornerstone of its economic reforms in this Parliament. The specific measures in this Act were foreshadowed by three White Papers: *'Productivity and Enterprise: A World Class Competition Regime'* (Cm 5233) and *'Productivity and Enterprise: Insolvency – A Second Chance'* (Cm 5234) published in July 2001, and *'Modern Markets: Confident Consumers'* (Cm 4410), published in July 1999.

16.   The main provisions of the Act are:

Competition reform
- A new merger regime, with decisions taken in most cases by independent competition authorities against a competition-based test rather than the current public interest test.

- Replacement of the monopoly regime established by the Fair Trading Act 1973 (FTA 1973) with a new regime for investigating markets. Most decisions will be taken by independent competition authorities against a competition-based test rather than the current public interest test.

- The introduction of criminal sanctions for individuals who engage in hard-core cartels.

- The OFT will be given a new power to apply for the court to disqualify directors involved in breaches of competition law.

- Persons harmed by a breach of competition law will be able to bring claims for damages before a specialist competition body (the Competition Appeal Tribunal (CAT)).

- Amendment to the Competition Act 1998 (CA 1998) to provide third parties with a direct right of appeal to the CAT against decisions of the OFT or the sectoral regulators with concurrent powers.

- Repeal of the arrangements for the exclusion of designated professional rules from the prohibitions under CA 1998.

Consumer reform

- Reform of Part III of FTA 1973 to extend the protection to consumers under the Stop Now Orders regime to those areas not covered by the Injunctions Directive.

- Repeal of most of Part II of FTA 1973, but with savings for two existing Orders made under this Part.

- Establishing a new regime for the OFT to approve business-to-consumer Codes of Practice.

- Requiring the OFT to respond in a set timescale to 'super-complaints' from designated consumer bodies.

- Requiring the OFT to provide information and advice which may include publication of educational materials.

Insolvency reform

Corporate insolvency

- Streamlining the administration procedure.

- Restricting the ability of lenders to appoint an administrative receiver to the holders of pre-existing floating charges and certain capital market and other transactions.

Crown Preference
- Removing the Crown's preferential rights in all insolvencies and making provision to ensure unsecured creditors are major beneficiaries.

Insolvency of individuals
- Providing for the automatic discharge of nearly all bankrupts after a maximum of 12 months.

- Reducing the number of restrictions that are automatically imposed on undischarged bankrupts.

- Providing for a court-based regime – Bankruptcy Restrictions Orders – to be attached to those bankrupts whose conduct, before and during bankruptcy, the court has found to be culpable.

Financial regime
- Enabling reform of the Insolvency Service financial regime, in particular, facilitating the return to creditors of more of the income from monies held in the Insolvency Services Investment Account.

COMMENTARY ON SECTIONS

17. The commentary on sections is set out by Part, with the commentary on the various Schedules included in that for the Part to which they relate. In these notes, the following abbreviations are used:

    - administrative receiver (AR);

    - bankruptcy restrictions orders (BROs);

    - bankruptcy restrictions undertakings (BRUs);

    - Company Directors Disqualification Act (CDDA 1986);

    - company voluntary agreement (CVA);

- Competition Act 1998 (CA 1998);

- Competition Appeal Tribunal (CAT);

- Competition Commission (CC);

- Control of Misleading Advertising Regulations 1988 (CMARS 1988);

- County Court Administration Orders (CCAOs);

- Criminal Justice Act 1987 (CJA 1987);

- Criminal Justice and Police Act 2001 (CJPA 2001);

- Department of Trade and Industry ("the Department");

- Director General of Fair Trading (DGFT);

- The treaty establishing the European Community (EC);

- Estate Agents Act 1979 (EAA 1979);

- European Community Merger Regulation (ECMR);

- Fair Trading Act 1973 (FTA 1973);

- insolvency practitioners (IPs);

- Office of Fair Trading (OFT);

- The Postal Services Commission (POSTCOMM);

- public-private partnership (PPP);

- Regulation of Investigatory Powers Act 2000 (RIPA 2000);

- Serious Fraud Office (SFO);

- Stop Now Orders (EC Directive) Regulations 2001 (SNORs);

- United Kingdom (UK);

- Water Industry Act 1991 (WIA 1991).

PART 1: THE OFFICE OF FAIR TRADING

Establishment etc. of Office of Fair Trading

Sections 1 and 2 & Schedule 1: The Office of Fair Trading & The Director General of Fair Trading

18.   Section 1 establishes a new corporate authority to be known as the OFT. Section 2 abolishes the office of DGFT and transfers the DGFT's functions, property, rights and liabilities to the OFT. The office of DGFT was established by FTA 1973. The DGFT has a wide range of functions in respect of consumer protection and competition matters.

19.   The OFT is to be a body corporate and is to consist of a Chairman and at least four other members. It is intended that the majority of members of the OFT to be non-executive appointments. As a Non-Ministerial Government Department, the OFT will be a Crown body and its staff will be civil servants.

20.   The organisation currently known as the OFT is not a statutory body, but simply the administrative support that has grown up around the DGFT to support him or her in the exercise of his or her statutory functions. The OFT name has also traditionally been used when publicising and explaining the work of the DGFT. References in the Act to the OFT are purely to the new corporate authority.

21.   In managing its affairs, the OFT is, under section 1, obliged to have regard to any relevant guidance on the governance of public bodies and to such generally accepted principles of good corporate governance as it is reasonable to regard as applicable to it. For example, the OFT would have to have regard to relevant principles in the Combined Code produced by the Hampel Committee on Corporate Governance in 1998.

22.   Schedule 1 sets out in more detail the OFT's internal structure. The Chairman is to be appointed by the Secretary of State. The other members are to be appointed by the Secretary of State in consultation with the Chairman. Members may be removed from office by the Secretary of State only on the grounds of incapacity or misbehaviour.

23.   The Secretary of State shall also, after consulting the Chairman, appoint a person to act as Chief Executive of the OFT. The Chief Executive may also be a member of the OFT. During the first two years after this provision comes into force, the Secretary of State may appoint a single person to hold both the post of Chairman and the post of Chief Executive. This is to provide some continuity for the OFT as the new arrangements settle down, and to allow the Government to honour its commitment to John Vickers. Mr Vickers will retire as Chairman and Chief Executive in 2005. The Schedule also gives the OFT the power to do anything that it thinks will facilitate or assist with the performance of its functions, and sets out its powers of delegation.

24.   Schedule 1 also requires the OFT to publish a summary of its rules and procedures for

dealing with conflicts of interest. It must consult the Secretary of State on these rules and procedures.

Section 3: Annual plan

25.   This section provides that the OFT will, before each financial year, publish an annual plan setting out its main objectives and priorities for the year ahead, and lay the plan before Parliament. It also obliges the OFT to consult on its proposals for the annual plan at least two months before publishing the final document, and to lay any consultation proposals before Parliament.

Section 4: Annual and other reports

26.   This section provides that, after the end of each financial year, the OFT will publish an annual report on its activities and performance, and lay the report before Parliament.

27.   *Subsection (2)* stipulates that each annual report will include a general survey of developments in respect of matters falling within the scope of the OFT's functions; an assessment of progress against the year's annual plan (see section 3); a summary of the OFT's significant decisions, investigations and activities; a break-down of how the OFT has allocated its resources; and an assessment of its enforcement activities. This is the minimum that must be included in the report; it is open to the OFT to include more information if it wishes.

28.   *Subsection (4)* allows the OFT to prepare other reports on issues that fall within its functions, and to publish them.

Schedule 24: Transitional and transitory provisions and savings

29.   This schedule contains various transitional provisions relating to the creation of the OFT, the abolition of the offices of the DGFT, and the repeal of Schedule 4 to the Competition Act 1998.

General functions of OFT

Section 5: Acquisition of information etc.

30.   This section gives the OFT the function of obtaining and reviewing information relating to any of its functions, both in respect of competition and consumer matters. This information-gathering role, which may involve research, is with a view to the OFT having the information it needs to make decisions and carry out its functions.

Section 6: Provision of information etc. to the public

31.   The OFT is given the function of promoting to the public the benefits that competition has for consumers and the economy. The OFT may also provide the public with information or advice on matters relating to its functions.

32.   In relation to these roles, the OFT may publish educational literature or take part in educational activities (such as seminars or lectures). It may also provide support to

others producing educational literature or carrying out educational activities.

33. In publishing information under sections 3, 4 and 6, OFT must have regard to the considerations set out in section 244. These are considering the need to exclude from disclosure: (i) any information whose disclosure OFT thinks is contrary to the public interest; (ii) commercial information whose disclosure OFT thinks might significantly harm the legitimate business interests of the undertaking to which it relates; and (iii) information relating to the private affairs of an individual whose disclosure OFT thinks might significantly harm the individual's interests. Under section 244, OFT must also consider the extent to which the disclosure of information mentioned under (ii) or (iii) above is necessary for the purpose of fulfilling its functions under sections 3, 4 and 6.

Section 7: Provision of information and advice to Ministers etc.

34. The OFT can, of its own volition, make proposals or give other information and advice to Government Ministers or public authorities on matters relating to its functions. Such advice may address the impact of future as well as existing legislation.

35. In addition to the OFT acting of its own volition, Government Ministers may also request proposals, information or advice from the OFT on matters relating to its functions.

Section 8: Promoting good consumer practice

36. This section enables the OFT to set up and undertake an enhanced role in respect of consumer codes of practice produced by a variety of bodies.

37. *Subsection (1)* sets out the OFT's general function to promote good practice in the carrying out of activities that may affect the economic interests of consumers in the UK.

38. *Subsection (2)* provides that the function includes making arrangements to approve consumer codes (as defined in subsection (6)) and both to give and withdraw approval.

39. It is expected that the OFT will use the power in this section to run a two-stage scheme under which bodies will submit their codes for approval. First, it is intended that bodies will develop consumer codes based on core criteria set by OFT. This first stage does not involve approval. OFT will confirm in writing where a code appears to meet the core criteria and is likely to be of practical benefit to consumers and good traders. At the second stage, sponsors will need to provide evidence of delivery of the initial promises in the code and the OFT will approve and promote the code once it is satisfied that this has been demonstrated. An approved code of practice will contain a redress mechanism and a complaints procedure. It might also include sector-specific criteria.

40. *Subsection (3)* provides that the arrangements made by OFT for approving consumer codes must set out the criteria it will use to decide whether approval should be granted or removed.

41. *Subsection (4)(a)* provides that the arrangements under subsection (2) may set out in detail the type of codes that may be the subject of an application for approval.

42. *Subsection (4)(b)* allows the OFT to set out arrangements for the use of a logo to signify OFT approval of a consumer code.

43. *Subsection (5)* requires OFT to publish the arrangements to approve consumer codes in any way it considers appropriate.

44. *Subsection (6)* defines a consumer code of practice as any document that is intended to regulate the conduct of a person supplying goods or services to consumers and the purpose of which is to safeguard or promote the interests of consumers. This definition does not include codes of practice that only give non-binding guidance.

Miscellaneous

Section 9: Repeal of certain powers of direction
45. This section repeals section 12 FTA 1973 and section 13 Competition Act 1980.

Section 10: Part 2 of the 1973 Act
46. Part II of FTA 1973 was created to allow the Secretary of State, on the advice of the DGFT and a then newly-created Consumer Protection Advisory Committee, to make orders to prevent or modify unfair (but not illegal) trade practices that harmed the economic interests of consumers. Only three orders have been made under Part II (of which two are still in force) and the Consumer Protection Advisory Committee, upon whose report the order-making power is dependent, has not existed in practice since 1983.

47. This section repeals most of Part II. It retains the two orders made under Part II that are still in force, and the enforcement provisions for those orders. It includes a power to repeal the remaining provisions of Part II once the two remaining orders have been revoked, and the enforcement provisions are therefore no longer required:

- *subsection (1)* repeals sections 3, 13–22 and Schedule 2 of FTA 1973;

- section 3 and Schedule 2 of FTA 1973 provide for the creation of the Consumer Protection Advisory Committee and set out the terms by which members of the Committee will be appointed and retained. They also set out the Committee's procedures for voting and arrangements for deputising for the Chairman. The Committee lost its quorum in 1982 and the last appointments expired in 1983;

- sections 13-16 FTA 1973 set out the role and duties of the Consumer Protection Advisory Committee. They set out the circumstances in which the Secretary of State, any other Minister, or the DGFT can ask the Committee to consider whether a specified consumer trade practice adversely affects the economic interests of consumers in the UK, and the requirements for the Committee to report on its findings;

- sections 17-21 FTA 1973 set out the circumstances in which the DGFT can, in a reference to the Advisory Committee, recommend that the Secretary of State makes an order to prevent a practice that is harming the economic interests of consumers from continuing. They also set out the requirements for the Committee to report on its findings;

- section 22 FTA 1973 gives the Secretary of State the power to make such an order following a recommendation by the Committee. Two orders made as a result of this provision remain in force today. These are the Consumer Transactions (Restrictions on Statements) Order 1976 (1976/1813 as amended by SI 1978/127) and the Business Advertisements (Disclosure) Order 1977 (1977/1918). No orders have been made under section 22 since then;

- The Consumer Transactions (Restrictions on Statements) Order 1976 makes it a criminal offence: (i) to use notices to attempt to restrict consumers' statutory rights, and (ii) to issue guarantees that do not mention that a consumer's statutory rights are not affected by the guarantee;

- The Business Advertisements (Disclosure) Order 1977 requires that anyone seeking to sell goods in the course of a business must ensure that any advertisements published make it reasonably clear that the goods are to be sold in the course of a business. An example of this in practice is where classified advertisements for car sales include a (T) where they are trade rather than private sales.

48. *Subsection (2)* provides that these two orders shall remain in force, notwithstanding the repeal of section 22 under which they were made. They will continue to be enforced under the provisions set out at sections 23-33 FTA 1973. The subsection also preserves the effect of section 22 so far as relating to any revocation of the orders. Accordingly, any revocation order will be subject to the affirmative resolution procedure.

49. *Subsection (3)* provides that, if and when those orders are revoked, the Secretary of State may repeal, by order, any remaining provisions of Part II of FTA 1973, and subsection (2) above, which will no longer be needed.

50. Subsection (3) allows for other consequential amendments or modifications that are necessary as a result of these repeals. *Subsection (4)* allows for transitional or savings

provisions to be made in connection with these. It also sets out that any orders under Subsection (3) will be made by negative resolution in either House of Parliament.

Section 11: Super-complaints to the OFT

51. This section gives certain designated consumer bodies the right to make a 'super-complaint' where they consider that there is any market feature or combination of features, such as the structure of a market or the conduct of those operating within it, that may be harming consumers to a significant extent. The market in question may be regional, national or supranational (where the UK forms part of that market). The aim of this procedure is to encourage groups who represent consumers to make relevant complaints on their collective behalf, and the OFT will be obliged to respond to a super-complaint within a specified time.

52. *Subsections (2) and (3)* set out the timeframe in which the OFT must respond. Within 90 days, the OFT will be required to make a considered response to a super-complaint, setting out what action, if any, it proposes to take under its competition or consumer powers. Eventual outcomes could, for example, include a formal reference to the CC or the publication by the OFT of a report recommending changes to regulation or self-regulation. The OFT must also explain the reasons behind its decision.

53. *Subsection (4)* allows the Secretary of State to alter the 90 day period for an OFT response should this period of time, through experience, prove to be either too lax or too limiting.

54. *Subsection (6)* provides for the route by which super-complainants will be named and describes who may qualify for super-complainant status: namely, those bodies who appear to represent the interests of consumers and meet the additional criteria for designation that the Secretary of State is required to publish.

55. *Subsection (7)* obliges the OFT to issue guidance on the presentation of a reasoned case. The OFT will of course require some evidence from the super-complainant in support of the super-complaint and super-complainants will expect to provide some supporting evidence. What constitutes a reasoned case will vary from case to case, but the OFT guidance will help super-complainants to submit a reasoned case. The OFT may also issue other relevant guidance, for example on the publicising of super-complaints or on super-complaints concerning the regulated sectors.

56. *Subsection (9)* cross-refers to the relevant definitions in Part 4 of the Act.

PART 2: THE COMPETITION APPEAL TRIBUNAL

The Competition Appeal Tribunal

Section 12: The Competition Appeal Tribunal

57.   This section creates the CAT. The CAT will take over the functions formerly performed by the appeal tribunals of the CC. Sections 17, 18, 19, 114, 120 and 179 of the Act give the CAT additional functions.

Schedule 2: The Competition Appeal Tribunal

58.   This Schedule sets out the terms of appointment to the CAT for the President, chairmen and ordinary members. The Lord Chancellor appoints the President and chairmen. The Secretary of State appoints ordinary members.

Section 13: The Competition Service

59.   This section establishes a new body called the Competition Service that will provide support services to the CAT. The Service will employ staff formerly employed by the Commission, and take on some of its assets and liabilities. Previously both the CC's inquiry panels and appeals tribunals were supported by the staff of the CC. This arrangement is no longer considered appropriate because the CAT will now hear appeals against decisions made by the CC.

Schedule 3: The Competition Service

60.   This Schedule establishes the Competition Service. The Service will consist of the President of the CAT, the Registrar of the CAT and one or more members appointed by the Secretary of State, and will have its own staff. Part 2 of the Schedule sets out the arrangements for transferring property, rights and liabilities from the CC to the Service.

Section 14: Constitution of Tribunal for particular proceedings and its decisions

61.   This section sets out the arrangements for proceedings before the CAT.

Section 15: Tribunal rules

62.   This section gives the Secretary of State the power to make the rules of the CAT.

Schedule 4: Tribunal: procedure

63.   Part 1 of this Schedule contains provisions concerning Tribunal decisions, and provides procedures for their enforcement. Paragraph 1 of this Schedule provides the procedure relating to decisions taken by the CAT. It contains similar provisions to those currently in paragraph 4 of Schedule 8 to CA 1998 (repealed by paragraph 8(5) of Schedule 5).

64.   Paragraphs 2-8 provide a procedure for the enforcement of certain decisions of the Tribunal that is distinct from the procedure for the enforcement of decisions of the OFT. At present, directions given by the CAT are enforced in the same way as OFT directions: thus the OFT must apply to the court under section 34 CA 1998 for an order requiring compliance with the CAT's direction. The new provisions provide a more direct means of enforcement, both of directions given by the CAT and awards of damages and costs.

65.   The new procedures permit most decisions of the CAT to be enforceable by

registration at the High Court in England and Wales, and by corresponding procedures in Scotland and Northern Ireland. By virtue of those procedures, the decision becomes enforceable in the same way as a judgment of the High Court (or, in Scotland, the Court of Session). However, penalties imposed by a decision of the CAT will continue to be enforced as a civil debt due to the OFT, under section 37 CA 1998.

66. Part 2 of Schedule 4 (paragraphs 2-25) sets out some of the areas that the Rules of the CAT may cover, and is based on the current Part II of Schedule 8 to the CA 98 (repealed by paragraph 8(5) of Schedule 5). New provisions have been added to take into account the CAT's new roles, including appeals on judicial review grounds (for cases under Part 3 and Part 4) and damages claims in competition cases. The CAT rules do not have to cover all of the areas mentioned, and can also cover issues that are not specified.

67. Part 2 includes provisions for rules to be made in relation to the rejection of proceedings by the CAT in various circumstances (subject to the parties being given the opportunity to be heard). These are, in cases other than damages claims, where the person bringing the proceedings does not have sufficient interest or shows no valid grounds; in the case of damages claims, where the CAT considers that there are no reasonable grounds for the claim or that a person bringing a representative claim is not entitled to do so; and in certain circumstances where the person bringing the proceedings has previously brought vexatious proceedings or made vexatious applications.

Section 16: Transfers of certain proceedings to Tribunal

68. Section 16 provides the Lord Chancellor with a power to make regulations allowing the courts - at their discretion - to transfer to the CAT matters arising in civil proceedings that require a determination of an infringement issue. An infringement issue is defined as any question relating to whether or not there has been an infringement of the prohibitions in Chapter I or Chapter II of CA 98 or the equivalent prohibitions in Articles 81 or 82 of the EC Treaty. *Subsection (3)* provides that rules of court may be made in connection with such a transfer. Any such rules would be made in line with the arrangements for drawing up rules of court in the different legal jurisdictions in the UK. ("Rules of court" has the meaning given by the schedule to the Interpretation Act 1978). Paragraph 25 of Schedule 4 specifies that Tribunal rules may make corresponding provision in connection with the transfer of proceedings from a court.

69. *Subsections (4) and (5)* allow the courts to transfer to the CAT so much of any proceedings as relate to a damages claim to which the new section 47A of the CA 98 apply (see below).

Proceedings under Part 1 of 1998 Act

Section 17: Third party appeals

70. This section replaces the existing section 47 CA 1998 by a new version that removes the current requirement for a third party first to request the OFT to withdraw or vary its decision before having a right of appeal to the CAT. For those purposes, a 'third party' is a person who is not a party to the agreement (or the author of the conduct) in respect of which the OFT has made its decision.

71. Section 47(1) specifies which decisions by the OFT may be appealed by a third party. The decisions covered are the same as in the existing version of section 47(1).

72. Section 47(2) specifies that a third party appeal may only be made by a person with sufficient interest or who represents persons with sufficient interest. This preserves the existing position, but responsibility for determining whether the party has sufficient interest will lie with the CAT and not the OFT as at present.

73. Section 47(3) preserves the existing position under the current section 47(7).

Section 18: Monetary Claims

74. *Subsection (1)* inserts a new section 47A in CA 1998 that will enable claims for damages, or other monetary awards, to be brought in the CAT (the CAT will also exercise the appeals jurisdiction currently exercised by the appeal tribunals of the CC, and the new review jurisdiction under Parts 3 and 4 of the Act). However, it will be possible to bring such claims in the CAT only where it has been established (by either the OFT or the European Commission) that an infringement of competition law has occurred. The right to bring such a claim will be without prejudice to the existing right to bring similar claims in the courts.

75. The new section 47A(1) and (3) enable the CAT to hear any claims for damages or other sums of money arising from a specified infringement of competition law, which could be made in civil proceedings before a court.

76. The new section 47A(6) specifies the infringements of competition law in respect of which a claim may be made to the CAT. These are: breaches of the prohibitions in Chapter I and Chapter II of CA 1998, and breaches of the prohibitions in Article 81 and Article 82 of the EC Treaty. Those prohibitions concern agreements, decisions and concerted practices that have the object or effect of preventing, restricting or distorting competition (Chapter I and Article 81), and conduct that amounts to the abuse of a dominant position (Chapter II and Article 82). Also included are existing decisions taken under the corresponding provisions of the European Coal and Steel Treaty, which expires on 23 July 2002.

77. The new section 47A(3) disapplies any limitation periods which would otherwise be applicable to such claims. The limitation periods for claims brought before the Tribunal will be specified in the CAT Rules.

78. The new section 47A(5), (6) and (8) further limit the claims that may be heard by the CAT. A claim may be brought only if it arises out of an infringement that has already

been established by a decision of the OFT, of the CAT itself on appeal from the OFT, or the European Commission. Except with the permission of the CAT, decisions are excluded that may still be subject to appeal (for instance an appeal to the CAT itself in the case of decisions of the OFT, to the Court of Appeal in the case of CAT decisions on such an appeal, or an application to the European Court of Justice in the case of decisions of the European Commission).

79. The new section 47A(9) makes it clear that, in determining the claim, the CAT is bound by the relevant decision establishing the infringement.

80. *Subsection (2)* provides that proceedings may be brought under the new section 47A in respect of claims arising before, as well as after, the commencement of that section. This will be subject to the limitation periods specified in the CAT Rules.

Section 19: Claims on behalf of consumers

81. This section inserts a new section 47B in CA 1998 that enables proceedings comprising claims for damages under section 47A to be brought in a representative capacity by a specified body on behalf of a group of named individual consumers.

82. The new section 47B(1) , (3) and (4) enable such claims to be made on behalf of any group of two or more consumers, provided that each consumer has given his or her consent, and the claims relate to the same infringement. 47B(3) also permits, under the same conditions, existing claims to be taken over by such a specified body. Such proceedings may only be made by a body that is specified by the Secretary of State under section 47B(9), and on behalf of persons who are claiming as consumers within the meaning given by sections 47B(2), (7) and (8). In particular, the infringement that is relied upon must affect goods or services that were received (or sought to be received) by the claimant otherwise than in the course of his or her business.

83. The new section 47B(6) provides that all sums awarded under this section must be awarded directly to the represented consumers, who will then be able to enforce the award in accordance with paragraphs 2 to 5 of Schedule 4. It also allows the CAT to order that the sum awarded be paid to the representative body who will then be able to enforce the award on behalf of the individuals in accordance with paragraphs 4(c) or 5(c) of Schedule 4. Such an order may only be made with the consent of both the individuals concerned and the representative body.

84. The new section 47B(7) and (8) sets out the conditions that must apply before an individual can be said to be a 'consumer' for the purposes of a consumer claim under this section. The infringement must have affected goods or services that the individual has received (or sought to receive) otherwise than in the course of business (although this will not exclude those received for the purposes of a future business). Conversely, the goods or services must have been supplied (or, had they been obtainable, would have been supplied) by a person acting in the course of business. A typical example will be where a consumer has bought goods for his or her own use, whose price has been inflated by a price-fixing agreement either among the suppliers

themselves, or the manufacturers, or possibly among the manufacturers' own suppliers.

85. The new section 47B(9) gives the Secretary of State the power to specify by order, and in accordance with published criteria, the bodies that are permitted to bring a representative claim. Such orders will be subject to negative Parliamentary procedure as specified in section 71 of the CA 1998.

86. The new section 47B(10) provides that a body wishing to be specified for the purposes of this section must make an application in a form approved by the Secretary of State.

Other amendments of the 1998 Act

Section 20: Findings of infringements
87. *Subsection (1)* inserts a new section 58A in CA 1998. The new section provides that certain decisions of the OFT or the CAT regarding an infringement of competition law are to bind the courts for the purpose of a subsequent claim for damages.

88. The new section 58A(1) specifies the infringements that are covered. These are: breaches of the prohibitions in Chapter I and Chapter II of CA 1998, and breaches of the prohibitions in Article 81 and Article 82 of the EC Treaty.

89. Subsection (2) clarifies that the new section 58A does not apply in relation to infringement decisions made before the commencement of the section. Decisions made before commencement will therefore not be binding on the courts when the courts are considering monetary claims.

Section 21 & Schedule 5: Proceedings under Part 1 of the 1998 Act
90. Schedule 5 makes a number of consequential amendments to CA 1998. It amends Schedule 7 to CA 1998 to remove references to the appeal tribunal. It also amends Schedule 8 to CA 1998 and section 49 CA 1998.

PART 3: MERGERS

Summary and Background
91. Part 3 of the Act makes reforms to the UK's regime for the control of mergers. It will replace the merger control provisions of FTA 1973, other than the special arrangements for the control of newspaper mergers, which will remain. Policy for merger reform has been developed through a programme of consultation that started in 1999. *'Mergers: A Consultation Document on Proposals for Reform'* (www2.dti.gov.uk/cp/mergercon/) was published in August 1999. *'Mergers: The Response to the Consultation on Proposals for Reform'* (www2.dti.gov.uk/cp/mergerresp/) was published in October 2000. The main proposals, together with some further refinements, were included in the *'Productivity*

and Enterprise: A World Class Competition Regime' White Paper published in July 2001.

92.   The main provisions of this Part of the Act provide for:

- final decisions on most mergers to be taken by the OFT and the CC rather than by the Secretary of State;

- mergers to be considered against a new test of whether they result in a substantial lessening of competition rather than the current, broader, public interest test;

- discretion for the competition authorities to clear a merger or allow it to proceed with less stringent competition remedies in circumstances where, notwithstanding an expected substantial lessening of competition, they expect it to result in defined types of customer benefit;

- the Secretary of State to continue to decide mergers which raise defined public interest considerations. National security is defined in the Act as such a consideration and there are powers for further such considerations to be defined by statutory instrument using the affirmative resolution procedure;

- revisions to the special regime for mergers between water enterprises to align it where possible with the general regime whilst preserving the importance currently attached to the ability of the water regulator to make comparisons between different enterprises;

- the retention of the existing two-stage approach to merger control. The OFT will carry out the first stage investigation to decide whether a reference to the CC is required. The CC will carry out the second stage, in-depth investigation where necessary;

- the retention of the UK's system of voluntary rather than compulsory pre-notification of mergers;

- statutory maximum timetables for competition authorities to reach final decisions for both first and second stage investigations;

- the replacement of the current worldwide assets-based criteria for determining whether a merger is subject to merger control procedures with a UK-based turnover test.

93.   The path of a merger investigation under the new system is summarised at Annex A.

Chapter 1: Duty to make references

Duty to make references: completed mergers

Section 22: Duty to make references in relation to completed mergers

94.   This section provides that the OFT must refer a completed merger to the CC for further investigation if certain circumstances arise. This differs from FTA 1973's arrangements for reference, where the Secretary of State has discretion to refer merger cases. This section will not apply to cases where the European Commission has exclusive jurisdiction to consider the competition aspects of the merger under the ECMR by virtue of the first paragraph of Article 21(2) ECMR.

95.   *Subsection (1)* provides that the OFT must make a reference to the CC if it believes there is or may be a 'relevant merger situation' that has or may be expected to result in a substantial lessening of competition. However, *subsection (2)* provides that the OFT can choose not to refer if it thinks either that the market involved is not of sufficient importance to justify a CC investigation, or that any substantial lessening of competition would be outweighed by benefits to customers.

96.   The OFT will be required under section 106 to publish advice and information on how these provisions will operate, and how it will apply the substantive tests. The substantial lessening of competition test, and the customer benefits concept are explained in more detail in the notes on sections 35 and 30 respectively.

97.   The discretion for the OFT to decide not to refer a merger because the market is of insufficient importance is designed primarily to avoid references being made where the costs involved would be disproportionate to the size of the markets concerned.

98.   *Subsection (3)* provides that the OFT is prevented from making a reference in each of the following circumstances:

  - the merger involves a newspaper transfer;

  - the OFT has accepted (or is considering accepting) undertakings in lieu of a reference in relation to the same transaction;

  - the merger was the subject of a 'merger notice' and the deadline for reference has passed;

  - the merger was referred to the CC before it was completed;

  - the merger raises a public interest consideration(s) and either an intervention notice is in force, or the case has been determined;

  - the merger is the subject of a request by the UK under Article 22(3) of the ECMR to the European Commission, and the European Commission is either

18

considering the request, proceeding with a case in pursuance of the request, or has dealt with the matter in response to the request.

99.   *Subsection (6)* provides that the definition of UK markets includes both sub-national and supra-national markets.

Section 23: Relevant merger situations

100.   This section sets out the criteria for a merger to qualify for investigation by the competition authorities, thereby making it a 'relevant merger situation'. It in substantial part reproduces sections 64 and 68 FTA 1973.

101.   It provides that a 'relevant merger situation' is created if: two or more enterprises have ceased to be distinct at a time or in circumstances set out in section 24, and at least one of the following thresholds is met:

- the value of the turnover in the UK of the enterprise being taken over exceeds £70m (the "turnover test"); or

- the merger would result in the creation or enhancement of at least a 25% share of supply of goods or services in the UK, or in a substantial part of the UK (the "share of supply" test). This would cover, for example, both the case of a merger between two enterprises each having a 15% share of supply, and that between two enterprises where one which already has a 25% share of supply mergers with another having a 5% share.

102.   The share of supply test is being retained from FTA 1973, but the turnover test is new, replacing an assets test. Section 123 gives the Secretary of State a power to amend the share of supply test.

103.   *Subsections (3) to (8)* make further provision as to the share of supply test. *Subsections (3) and (4)* enable the test to be applied to the net share of goods or services supplied by or to the merging enterprises. *Subsection (5)* allows the authorities to apply such criteria (such as value, cost, quantity, etc) as they consider appropriate to determine whether the 25% threshold is satisfied, and *subsections (6) and (7)* allow the authorities to consider whether goods or services subject to different forms of supply should be aggregated for this purpose. *Subsection (8)* gives the competition authorities the discretion to decide whether goods or services are to be treated as goods or services of a separate description for this purpose.

104.   *Subsection (9)* has the effect that the question of whether there is a relevant merger situation is to be determined immediately before the time when the reference has been, or is to be made, except in circumstances where the CC has decided to treat the reference of an anticipated merger as that of a completed merger by virtue of section 36(2), when it is to be determined as at such time as the CC may determine.

Section 24: Time-limits and prior notice

105. This section provides for the time period in which completed mergers may be treated as a 'relevant merger situation' and are therefore referable. These re-enact those applying under FTA 1973.

106. A reference to the CC must be made within four months of the completion of a merger, or (if later) material facts about the merger being made public or given to OFT.

107. For this purpose, the section defines the term 'made public' as having the meaning of 'generally known or readily ascertainable'. The intention is that OFT would reasonably be expected to have known or found out about the merger if it has not been notified about it.

Section 25: Extension of time-limits

108. This section allows for the extension of the four-month period in which a merger can be referred in certain circumstances: where the OFT and parties have agreed an extension; where parties have failed to provide information to the OFT as requested; where undertakings are being sought; or where the UK has made a request to the EC under article 22(3) of the ECMR. Where there are multiple extensions, there is provision for the extensions to run concurrently where it is sensible to count the time period in this way.

Section 26: Enterprises ceasing to be distinct enterprises

109. This section defines a merger situation. It is closely modelled on section 65 FTA 1973, with one omission to take account of the existence of CA 1998.

110. The provision in 65(1)(b) of FTA 1973 that referred to 'arrangements entered into in order to prevent competition between enterprises' has been omitted. Where such arrangements do not fall within the merger regime under the Enterprise Act 2002, it is considered they will be better suited to investigation under CA 1998.

111. *Subsection (1)* defines 'two enterprises ceasing to be distinct' by reference to whether they are brought under common ownership or common control.

112. An 'enterprise' is defined in section 129 as the activities, or part of the activities, of a business; and a 'business' is defined to include a professional practice and to include any other undertaking that is carried on for gain or reward or that is an undertaking in the course of which goods or services are supplied other than free of charge. The definition includes 'part of the activities of a business' as it is sometimes an operating division of a company that is acquired rather than the whole of the company.

113. *Subsections (3) and (4)* (which are modelled on the equivalent FTA 1973 provisions) envisage three levels of control of an enterprise. These are: material influence over policy; control of policy (often called *de facto* control); and a controlling interest in the enterprise (often called *de jure* control). What constitutes material influence or control will be considered on a case-by-case basis by the competition authorities

according to the particular circumstances of the case. Under the FTA the authorities have treated the acquisition of the ability to appoint a director or having a 15% shareholding as sufficient to give material influence for these purposes. *De facto* and *de jure* control will arise at higher levels of shareholding, with *de jure* normally requiring more than 50% of the voting rights.

114.   Two enterprises cease to be distinct when there is an increase in the level of control - see section 26(3), (4)(a) and (4)(b). It is thus possible for a merger situation to be investigated at any of the three points where there is an increase in the level of control if the different levels of control are acquired at different times.

Sections 27 and 29: Time when enterprises cease to be distinct & Obtaining control by stages

115.   Sections 27 and 29 reproduce sections 69 and 66A FTA 1973. These provide for the application of merger control to cases where ownership or control of an enterprise is obtained over a period of time. The key rule is contained in section 27(2), namely that mergers are treated as having been completed at the moment when all the parties to a transaction are contractually bound to do so. It makes clear that no account is to be taken of options that have not been exercised or conditional rights where the conditions have not been satisfied.

116.   Section 27(5) to (8) deals with certain cases where ownership or control has been acquired incrementally over a period of time. Where this has been achieved through one or successive transactions or arrangements between the same parties or interests, the competition authorities can treat them as having all occurred on the date of the last relevant event, subject to a two-year cut-off period.

117.   Section 29 allows the authorities to treat a series of separate transactions over a period of up to two years, under which a person or group of persons acquire control of an enterprise, to be treated as occurring on the date of the last transaction when considering a reference. Unlike under section 27, there is no need for the transactions to be linked, nor for them to be between the same persons.

Section 28: Turnover test

118.   This section provides for how the turnover test, which will replace the current 'assets test' contained in sections 64 and 67 FTA 1973, is to be determined. The test will apply to turnover in the UK, and will be set initially at £70 million, but this figure will be alterable by statutory instrument.

119.   The test will be determined by reference to the turnover of the enterprise being taken over (i.e. if the turnover of the target company exceeds £70 million, the merger qualifies for investigation). If it is the case that no enterprise will continue under the same ownership after the merger (for example, formation of a new joint venture), the turnover for the purposes of the test is to be calculated by aggregating that of all the enterprises involved, and taking away the highest. The section also provides that the OFT shall keep the figure under review, and from time to time advise the Secretary of

State if it is still an appropriate level.

120.   Section 28(2) provides the Secretary of State with a power to make an order with respect to how the turnover in the UK of an enterprise is to be calculated, which may, in particular, make provision for the amounts which are to be taken into account, the dates by reference to which it is to be determined and the connection of that turnover with the UK.

Section 30: Relevant customer benefits

121.   This section defines the benefits to customers that the authorities can take into account. They are benefits in the form of lower prices, greater innovation, greater choice or higher quality in a UK market. Customer benefits may be relevant to decisions of the OFT and the CC in two main situations:

- the OFT has a duty to refer mergers that it believes may result in a substantial lessening of competition, with some limited exceptions. One of the circumstances where the OFT may decide not to refer is where it expects customer benefits to outweigh the substantial lessening of competition;

- if a merger is referred, the CC is required to determine whether a merger will result in a substantial lessening of competition. If the CC makes such a determination, it has a duty to apply remedies. At the stage when the CC is deciding on remedies, the Act enables it, in particular, to have regard to customer benefits (see note on section 41). The CC will have scope to apply lesser competition remedies than would otherwise be the case. This scope would extend, at one extreme, to clearing a merger without any conditions if the customer benefits are of sufficient importance and nothing can be done about the competition problems without eliminating the relevant customer benefit that the CC wishes to recognise.

122.   Relevant customer benefits are narrowly defined. They are not expected to arise very often. They must be in the form of lower prices, greater innovation, greater choice or higher quality in a UK market. This definition is related to the competition test because the benefits are ones that would normally be expected to arise in a fully competitive market.

123.   The definition is further narrowed in the following ways:

- the authority has to have an expectation that the benefits will be realised within a reasonable time-frame as a result of the merger;

- the authority has to consider that the benefits are unlikely to arise without the merger (unless the only other ways of realising the customer benefit would have a similarly detrimental effect on competition);

- relevant customers are limited to the customers of the merged or merging entity. The term also extends to other customers provided they are in a chain of customers beginning with the immediate customers of the merging entity. In both cases, the term extends to future customers because in some circumstances a merger can lead to the development of new products or services and the creation of new markets.

124. Both the OFT and the CC will be required to produce information and advice respectively about the making and consideration of references. This will include information and advice about their application of the customer benefits concept. Examples of mergers that might – depending on the specific circumstances – generate customer benefits that could be taken into account by the OFT in deciding whether to make a reference, or by the CC in determining remedies, are as follows:

- a merger producing so-called 'network benefits'. A merger might give customers of one enterprise improved access to a wider network operated by the other enterprise, with the wider choice of complementary products that this brings. For example, in mobile telecommunications, the more users who join a particular mobile network, the more valuable the network becomes to those users as they can contact more people, in more locations, at lower cost as the network increases. In the transport sector, network benefits can improve service quality through strengthened hubs, better through-ticketing arrangements or better-connected services;

- mergers leading to large economies of scale where the effect of scale economies on prices is sufficient to outweigh the effect of a substantial lessening of competition. Such circumstances could lead to an overall reduction in prices and be beneficial to both consumers and business, provided that the authorities were satisfied that the economies of scale would be realised in spite of a significant reduction in competition and that prices after the merger would remain lower than they were pre-merger;

- mergers producing more innovation through research and development benefits. Investment in research and development often involves large fixed costs and there may be circumstances where critical mass is needed – in terms of research expertise or capital or both – that can only be secured through a merger.

125. These examples are illustrative only, and should not be regarded as pre-judging what may or may not be included in the advice published by the competition authorities.

Section 31: Information powers in relation to completed mergers

126. This section sets out a new procedure for the OFT to obtain information from the parties of a possible completed merger. It allows the OFT to require information by notice, and provides that the notice must tell the parties what information is required,

when it is required and what may happen if the parties do not comply with such a request (i.e. a reference to the CC).

Section 32: Supplementary provision for purposes of sections 25 and 31

127. This section provides the Secretary of State with a power to make regulations about the operation of the extension of the OFT's timetable for reference or the OFT's information-gathering powers in relation to completed mergers. The section also sets out arrangements for certain notices extending the four-month period.

Duty to make references: anticipated mergers

Section 33: Duty to make references in relation to anticipated mergers

128. This section provides that the OFT must refer an anticipated merger (i.e. one that has not yet taken place) to the CC for further investigation in certain circumstances. It broadly mirrors the reference duty in section 22. However, because there may be some uncertainty in these cases about whether a merger will go ahead, the OFT is given discretion not to refer unless it believes the proposals are sufficiently far advanced or likely to proceed. The OFT will cover this point in its published guidance.

Section 34: Supplementary provision in relation to anticipated mergers

129. This section provides a power for the Secretary of State to make provision about the operation of sections 27 and 29 in relation to anticipated mergers and public interest intervention notices relating to them.

Determination of references

Sections 35–41

130. These sections set out the functions and duties of the CC once a merger has been referred to it. The sections have similarities with existing provisions in FTA 1973, but reflect the removal of Ministers from the decision-making process, the new status of the CC as the determinative body in all cases other than ones raising defined public interest considerations, and the switch from a 'public interest' test to a 'substantial lessening of competition' test for the assessment of mergers.

Section 35: Questions to be decided in relation to completed mergers

131. This section sets out the questions that the CC has to decide as part of a reference. Its first task is to decide whether a relevant merger situation has been created. In doing so, it is confirming (or otherwise) the OFT's initial belief in making a reference under section 22 that a relevant merger situation has been created. If it has, the CC has to decide whether the merger has resulted, or will result, in a substantial lessening of competition. This competition-based test will be the central provision of the new regime. It replaces the public interest test in section 84 FTA 1973. In general, under the new regime, the CC will only have grounds for remedial action if the CC finds that the merger has resulted or may be expected to result in a substantial lessening of competition. (The only exception to this will be in certain public interest cases

considered under the procedure set out in Chapter 2.)

132.   The term 'substantial lessening of competition' is not defined in the Act. However, it is intended that advice and information on the operation of the competition test will be provided by the CC (and the OFT) under section 106. This requires the competition authorities to publish general advice and information about how they will consider references and how the relevant provisions will operate.

133.   The concept of a substantial lessening of competition and its application in the context of a reference inquiry will be for the CC to explain in detail in its guidance. Similar language is used in the legislation controlling mergers in a number of other major jurisdictions, including the US, Canada, Australia and New Zealand. The concept is an economic one, best understood by reference to the question of whether a merger will increase or facilitate the exercise of market power (whether unilateral, or through co-ordinated behaviour), leading to reduced output, higher prices, less innovation or lower quality or choice. A number of matters may be potentially relevant to the assessment of whether a merger will result in a substantial lessening of competition. The matters may include, but are not limited to:

- market shares and concentration;

- extent of effective competition before and after the merger;

- efficiency and financial performance of firms in the market;

- barriers to entry and expansion in the relevant market;

- availability of substitute products and the scope for supply- or demand-side substitution;

- extent of change and innovation in a market;

- whether in the absence of the merger one of the firms would fail and, if so, whether its failure would cause the assets of that firm to exit the market;

- the conduct of customers or of suppliers to those in the market.

134.   If the CC decides that there is a substantial lessening of competition, it is also required to decide whether to take action to remedy, mitigate or prevent the substantial lessening of competition or any adverse effects resulting from that loss of competition. Adverse effects in this context are the undesirable consequences that flow from the loss of competition such as higher prices or reduced choice for customers. In deciding what action should be taken, however, *subsection (4)* requires the CC to achieve as comprehensive a solution as is reasonable and practicable to the substantial lessening of competition and the adverse effects resulting from it. The

reference to a 'comprehensive solution' will require the CC to consider remedies that address the substantial lessening of competition itself (e.g. the features arising from the merger that give rise to the creation of market power) because it is generally more effective to tackle the cause of any problems at their source rather than by tackling the symptoms or adverse effects.

135. This section is closely linked with section 41, which sets out the factors that the CC must or may in particular bear in mind in choosing remedies.

136. *Subsections (6) and (7)* allow the OFT to frame references in a way that requires the CC to limit the questions that it has to consider in deciding whether a relevant merger situation has been created. For example, the reference can be framed in a way that does not require the CC to consider whether the turnover of the enterprise being acquired is over the relevant turnover threshold. In those circumstances, it would consider only whether the share of supply test had been met. Conversely, it can be asked to consider only whether the turnover threshold has been met. The CC can also be required to limit its consideration of whether the share of supply test has been met to a particular part of the UK.

Section 36: Questions to be decided in relation to anticipated mergers

137. This section is the equivalent to section 35. It sets out the questions that the CC has to decide when an anticipated merger (a merger that is in progress or contemplation) has been referred. The questions are similar, but with a future tense used where appropriate to reflect the fact that the merger has not yet been completed.

Section 37: Cancellation and variation of references under section 22 or 33

138. The section allows the OFT to vary a merger reference once it has been made, although this does not carry with it a power to alter the period within which the CC is required to report. It is based on section 71 FTA 1973. The circumstances where this flexibility might be required include situations where the parties have been identified incorrectly, or the grounds for the original reference were wrong.

139. The section introduces a provision giving the CC a new power to change the type of reference made, where the facts justify it. The power might be used, for example, where a merger is referred as an anticipated merger under section 32, but is subsequently completed.

Section 38: Investigations and reports on references under section 22 or 33

140. This section gives the CC an obligation to publish a report on each of its merger references within the statutory time-limit (see below). The section is closely modelled on section 72 FTA 1973 but with differences reflecting the determinative role of the CC both in relation to decisions on the competition test and decisions on what remedies to apply. The section includes a requirement for the CC to give reasons for its decision and information allowing for a proper understanding of the decisions.

Section 39: Time-limits for investigations and reports

141. Section 70 FTA 1973 currently requires the Secretary of State to set a timetable within which the CC has to report. That timetable cannot exceed 6 months. The period set is extendable for one further period of up to 3 months where the Secretary of State is satisfied that there are special reasons why the report cannot be made within the initial period.

142. Section 39 replaces section 70 FTA 1973. It requires the CC to publish its report on a reference within a statutory maximum period of 24 weeks from the date of reference. A shorter period applies if that is needed to comply with Article 9(6) of the ECMR in circumstances where a merger has been referred back for consideration by the UK domestic competition authorities.

143. The section permits the CC to extend the 24-week period for the report for one further period of no more than 8 weeks where it is satisfied that there are special reasons for a delay. The section does not further define 'special reasons', but it is anticipated that they would include matters such as the illness or incapacity of members of a reporting group that has seriously impeded its work, and an unexpected event such as a merger of competitors.

144. An important difference between the current FTA 1973 timetable and the proposed new timetable is that the CC's report will have to contain not only its decisions on the substantive question of whether there is expected to be a substantial lessening of competition, but also its decisions on remedies. At present, the CC makes the substantive finding against a public interest test, but only makes recommendations to the Secretary of State about the remedies that might be appropriate. The Secretary of State has an unlimited period within which to take final decisions on remedies.

145. *Subsection (4)* gives the CC a discretion that it does not have in the current regime to extend the period within which it has to report where one of the parties to a merger (but not third parties) has failed to comply with a formal notice (see section 109) requiring the provision of information or documents, or the appearance of witnesses. Any such extension continues until the information is provided, or the CC decides to cancel the extension.

Section 40: Section 39: supplementary

146. This section gives the Secretary of State a power by order to shorten the maximum statutory timetable of 24 weeks, and the maximum 8 week period for any extension. They can be lengthened again if necessary, but in no circumstances can the periods be extended beyond 24 weeks and 8 weeks respectively. The section also gives the Secretary of State a power to make regulations covering detailed procedural matters connected with the provision of information and documents, such as the time at which information is to be treated as having been provided.

Section 41: Duty to remedy effects of completed or anticipated mergers

147. There are close links between this section and sections 36 and 37. The latter require the CC to decide whether a merger has or may be expected to result in a substantial

lessening of competition, and to identify any action that should be taken to address it. Section 41 requires the CC to take the action that it considers to be reasonable and practicable to remedy, mitigate or prevent the competition problems that it has identified. The steps have to be consistent with the course of action included in the report on the reference, unless there has been a material change of circumstances, or the CC has a special reason for taking different steps.

148. The CC has a choice of preventing, remedying or mitigating the substantial lessening of competition or the adverse effects arising from that loss of competition. However, it has to have particular regard to the need to achieve as comprehensive a solution as is reasonable and practicable to the substantial lessening of competition itself.

149. *Subsection (5)* gives the CC an express discretion, in deciding on what action to take to address the competition problems, to have regard to the effect of any such action on any relevant customer benefits (as defined in section 30). The purpose of this subsection is to ensure that the CC has scope, if it considers that customer benefits are of sufficient importance, to impose a lesser competition remedy or no remedy at all if the only steps that the CC could take to remedy the competition problem are steps that would mean that the customer benefits could not be realised.

Chapter 2: Public interest cases

150. Sections 42-58 set out the regime for the investigation of mergers that raise matters of public interest in addition to, or instead of, competition and customer benefit concerns. In future, such matters may only be investigated and taken into account if the Secretary of State intervenes in a case. The flowchart at Annex B illustrates the handling of these cases.

Power to make references

Section 42: Intervention by Secretary of State in certain public interest cases
151. This section allows the Secretary of State to intervene in the consideration of a case by serving an intervention notice where she believes it raises a public interest consideration that needs to be taken into account.

152. *Subsection (2)* allows the Secretary of State to serve an intervention notice in a case that she thinks might raise one or more public interest considerations, and *subsection (4)* provides that only one intervention notice may be served in any case. *Subsection (3)* limits the considerations that she may raise in this way to those specified in section 58 or those that the Secretary of State thinks should be so specified. *Subsection (7)* has the effect that, in the latter case, the Secretary of State must bring forward an order specifying the consideration in legislation and seeking Parliament's approval of it ('finalise' the consideration) as early as practicable.

153. *Subsection (1)* sets out the conditions to be met before an intervention notice can be served. A key condition is that the notice cannot be served if a reference decision has

already been taken by OFT.

Section 43: Intervention notices under section 42

154. This section sets out that the intervention notice must include certain details, including which case it relates to, and which public interest considerations may be relevant. It provides that, where the Secretary of State believes that more than one public interest consideration may be relevant, she has discretion not to mention such of them in the intervention notice as she considers appropriate. The section also provides that an intervention notice will come into force as soon as it is given, and that it will cease to be in force once the role of the Secretary of State in relation to that case is complete (either because she has acted or is prevented from acting by the legislation).

Section 44: Investigation and report by OFT

155. This section sets out the duties of the OFT to report to the Secretary of State in a case where an intervention notice has been served.

156. *Subsection (2)* provides that the OFT will report to the Secretary of State within a deadline set by the Secretary of State. There is nothing to prevent the Secretary of State from altering the deadline if circumstances so require.

157. *Subsections (3)–(7)* ensure that the Secretary of State will receive information on at least two areas:

- the OFT's advice on any competition issues (including customer benefits, the importance of the market and the scope for undertakings-in-lieu if relevant), as well as its view on whether a relevant merger situation has or would be created; and

- the OFT's summary of the representations that it has received in relation to the public interest considerations mentioned in the intervention notice.

Section 45: Power of Secretary of State to refer matter to Commission

158. This section allows the Secretary of State to make the decision on whether a merger raising public interest considerations should be referred to the CC.

159. *Subsection (1)* ensures that the Secretary of State only has the power to refer a case if there is an intervention order in force relating to that case and the OFT has produced a report on that case for the Secretary of State.

160. *Subsections (2)–(7)* provide that the Secretary of State may make a reference if she believes that there could be a 'relevant merger situation' that might be adverse to the public interest. In deciding whether to make a reference, she will be bound to accept the views of OFT on any competition-related issues, but may also have regard to the public interest considerations cited in the intervention notice.

161. Thus *subsection (6)* ensures that the Secretary of State will view a competition problem identified by the OFT as being adverse to the public interest unless she considers this to be outweighed in the overall assessment.

Section 46: References under section 45: supplementary

162. This section further qualifies the Secretary of State's power to refer under section 45. As with the OFT's duties to refer under sections 22 and 33, no reference is permitted if the merger involves a newspaper transfer, or was the subject of either accepted undertakings in lieu of a reference or a merger notice if the deadline for reference has passed. In addition, this section prevents the Secretary of State from clearing a merger where the OFT identified competition concerns if the public interest consideration(s) that she wishes to base that decision on had not been approved by Parliament. The Secretary of State may delay taking the decision on reference for up to 24 weeks from the date of the intervention notice so that she might be able to take a newly-approved consideration into account.

Reports on references

Section 47: Questions to be decided on references under section 45

163. This section sets out the matters that the CC must decide in the case of a reference by the Secretary of State.

164. *Subsections (1) and (4)* provide that, as in all cases, the CC must first decide whether a 'relevant merger situation' has been created, or is in the process of being created. If so, *subsections (2), (3), (5) and (6)* provide for it to reach a view on whether it considers the merger would be adverse overall to the public interest and, if relevant to the reference, would result in a substantial lessening of competition. *Subsections (7)-(10)* ensure that the CC will consider how any of those problems might be remedied, mitigated or prevented.

Section 48: Cases where references or certain questions need not be decided

165. This section provides that, in certain circumstances, the CC need not decide certain questions in relation to a case that raises public interest considerations.

166. *Subsection (1)* provides for the CC to cancel a reference in relation to an anticipated merger where it believes that the arrangements for that merger transaction have been abandoned. *Subsections (2) and (3)* allow the Secretary of State to frame references in a way that requires the CC to limit the questions that it has to consider in deciding whether a relevant merger situation has been or will be created.

Section 49: Variation of references under section 45

167. This section ensures that a qualifying merger situation referred as an anticipated merger may be handled by the CC as a completed merger, and vice versa. The section also provides for the Secretary of State to vary a reference, but any variation must not alter the time available to the CC to make its report or the public interest consideration

specified in the reference.

Section 50: Investigations and reports on references under section 45

168.   This section provides that the CC will prepare a report for the Secretary of State on any reference made to it under section 45.

169.   *Subsection (1)* provides that the CC will have the same deadline for producing a report for the Secretary of State on a case raising a public interest concern as it would have to produce and publish its report on a competition-only case (i.e. within 24 weeks).

170.   *Subsections (2) and (3)* provide for the CC to give a general report on the subject of the merger and to report on whether there was either a completed or anticipated merger. If so, the CC would report on whether the transaction could be expected to operate against the public interest, and (where the reference has been made on competition and public interest grounds) whether the transaction could be expected to result in a substantial lessening of competition. If either or both of these findings were adverse, the report should also contain advice on how to remedy, prevent or mitigate identified adverse effects. The CC will have to give reasons for its conclusions.

Section 51: Time-limits for investigations and reports by Commission

171.   This section (*subsection (1)*) provides for an upper time-limit of 24 weeks for the CC to send its report to the Secretary of State in a case raising public interest concerns. FTA 1973 currently sets a time-limit of six months. *Subsection (2)* ensures that, where the merger has been referred back to the UK from the European Commission, the CC will report within a shorter time-limit if necessary.

172.   *Subsections (3)-(8)* provide for extensions to the 24-week timetable. The CC may extend the timetable once by up to 8 weeks where it has special reasons to do so. FTA 1973 currently allows an extension of up to 3 months. The CC will also be able to extend the timetable where a party to the merger fails to deliver required information – the extension in those cases would be for the period between the deadline for receipt of the information and the actual receipt of that information, or until the CC cancelled the extension.

Section 52: Section 51: supplementary

173.   This section limits the ability of the CC to extend its timetable in a case that has been referred back to the UK, where that would conflict with the timetable set by the ECMR. It also provides that the extensions provided for special circumstances and delays in obtaining information can be cumulative, but that multiple extensions for failure to provide information can run concurrently where they overlap. The section also allows the Secretary of State to alter the standard timetable and extension time-periods (but provides that the periods must not be set above 24 weeks and 8 weeks respectively).

Section 53: Restrictions on action where public interest considerations not finalised

174.   This section provides that the CC will only continue to consider a public interest consideration cited in a relevant intervention notice where it has previously been approved by Parliament (either in the Act, or subsequently), or is so approved within 24 weeks of the serving of the intervention notice in the case.

175.   In a case raising a new public interest consideration, the CC will not report to the Secretary of State, unless either Parliament has approved the creation of a new public interest consideration, or a period of 24 weeks has passed since the serving of the intervention notice, or the case is subject to the ECMR timetable. In any case, the CC will disregard any public interest consideration that is not finalised at the time it gives its report to the Secretary of State.

Decisions of the Secretary of State

Section 54: Decision of Secretary of State in public interest cases

176.   This section sets out how the Secretary of State will proceed on receipt of a report from the CC in a case raising any public interest consideration(s).

177.   *Subsection (3)* provides for the circumstances in which the Secretary of State can make an adverse public interest finding. *Subsection (4)* provides that the Secretary of State may decide not to make any finding on the adverse public interest test if she thinks that no public interest consideration is relevant to the case. *Subsection (5)* ensures that the Secretary of State must make her decision within 30 days from receipt of the CC's report.

178.   *Subsection (6)* ensures that the Secretary of State will take account only of any public interest considerations that were specified in the reference and were not disregarded by the CC for its report. *Subsection (7)* provides that the Secretary of State cannot diverge from the relevant competition authority's conclusion on competition.

Section 55: Enforcement action by Secretary of State

179.   This section provides that the Secretary of State may accept undertakings from or impose orders on the parties to address any of the adverse effects she has identified where she has made an adverse public interest finding. *Subsection (2)* provides that she may only take steps provided for in paragraphs 9 and 11 of Schedule 7. *Subsections (3) and (4)* provide that, in making her decisions on enforcement, the Secretary of State shall have regard to the views of the CC presented in its report and may take account of any customer benefits where there has been a substantial lessening of competition.

Other

Section 56: Competition cases where intervention on public interest grounds ceases

180.   This section provides for a case to revert to the competition authorities for a decision where an intervention notice ceases to have effect, either because of the Secretary of State deciding that the public interest consideration is not relevant to the case, or, in a case where parliamentary approval of the consideration is required, that approval is not given within the 24-week period mentioned above.

181.   *Subsection*s *(1) and (2)* provide for the Secretary of State to hand a case back to the OFT for a decision on reference where she decides the public interest consideration(s) cited in the intervention notice are irrelevant to the case.

182.   *Subsections (3)-(5)* provide for the CC to revert to a competition-only investigation where the relevant intervention notice has ceased to be in force. The CC is to have the same timetable for producing and publishing its report as it had been granted for producing a report for the Secretary of State, plus an additional 20 working days.

183.   *Subsection (6)* provides for the CC to proceed as though it had conducted and published a report on a competition-only investigation where the Secretary of State decides that no public interest consideration is relevant to the case.

Section 57: Duties of OFT and Commission to inform Secretary of State

184.   This section ensures that the OFT and the Commission pass relevant information to the Secretary of State.

185.   *Subsection (1)* provides that the OFT will inform the Secretary of State if it believes that any case it is considering raises any public interest consideration already specified in legislation that the Secretary of State would not consider immaterial.

186.   *Subsection (2)* provides that the OFT and the CC must pass on to the Secretary of State any representations that they receive about the need for the Secretary of State to specify a new public interest consideration.

Section 58: Specified considerations

187.   This section sets out the considerations that may need to be looked at alongside competition matters in merger cases. It also provides a mechanism for varying the specified considerations.

188.   *Subsection (1)* provides that 'national security' is the only consideration specified.

189.   *Subsection*s *(3) and (4)* provide that the public interest considerations specified may be added to, removed or amended and that the revised considerations may be used in any case, regardless of the progress of the order amending the considerations.

Chapter 3: Other special cases

Special public interest cases

190.   These sections provide for an exceptional category of mergers that may be referred for investigation on public interest grounds, even though they do not meet the normal qualifying thresholds (the turnover test or the share of supply test). These include mergers involving certain government contractors (or subcontractors) who may hold or receive confidential information or material relating to defence.

191.   They will not be scrutinised on competition grounds, but against public interest considerations only.

Section 59: Intervention by Secretary of State in special public interest cases

192.   *Subsection (1)* provides that the Secretary of State may intervene on special public interest grounds if she has reasonable grounds for suspecting that: a special merger situation has been created or is in contemplation. *Subsection (2)* provides that the Secretary of State may issue a special intervention notice if she believes that the case raises public interest considerations as specified in section 58.

193.   *Subsection (3)* provides that a special merger situation is one where the usual thresholds of share of supply or turnover have not been met and the conditions in *subsection (4)* are satisfied. Those conditions are that one of the enterprises is carried on in the UK, or by or under control of a body corporate incorporated in the UK and a person carrying on one of the enterprises is a relevant government contractor. *Subsections (5) and (6)* provide that for the purposes or determining whether a relevant merger situation has been created, sections 22-31 shall apply, subject to certain changes listed in *subsection (6)*. These changes clarify that certain references to the OFT shall, for the purposes of the Chapter, be read as the Secretary of State.

194.   *Subsection (8)* defines a relevant government contractor as a contractor whose contract includes handling confidential information or documents. They are notified of this by the Secretary of State, or on behalf of the Secretary of State in cases where this notification is passed on from a prime to a subcontractor. This subsection also establishes that a relevant government contractor includes a former contractor whose notification has not been revoked.

195.   *Subsection (9)* defines defence as having the same meaning as in section 2 of the Official Secrets Act 1989, and further defines government contractor as having the meaning given in the 1989 Act and including subcontractors.

Section 60: Special intervention notices under section 59

196.   This section provides that a special intervention notice shall contain details of the case concerned, and the public interest considerations specified in section 58 which are thought to be relevant. It also provides for the circumstances in which a special intervention notice would finally be determined and the time at which it would be determined.

Section 61: Initial investigation and report by OFT

197.   This section establishes the OFT's role in investigating and reporting on these cases.

Subsections (1) and (2) establish that if the Secretary of State issues a special intervention notice to OFT, they shall produce a report within such time-limit as the Secretary of State may require. There is nothing to prevent the Secretary of State from altering the time-limit if circumstances so require. *Subsection (3)* provides that, in its report, the OFT will consider matters relevant to references under sections 22 and 33 which are also relevant to the criteria specified in section 62. This means that OFT do not need to consider whether the merger may result in a substantial lessening of competition as this is not relevant to the Secretary of State's decision in a special public interest case. This subsection also provides that the OFT's report will include a summary of representations received that are relevant to the Secretary of State's decision.

198. *Subsection (4)* provides that the OFT shall decide whether a special merger situation has been created or is contemplated. This will be a relevant merger situation without the need to meet the qualifying thresholds (share of supply or turnover test). *Subsection (5)* provides that OFT may, at its discretion, provide other advice that may be relevant to the Secretary of State's decision about whether to refer, and *subsection (6)* allows the OFT to carry out their investigations for the report as it considers appropriate.

Section 62: Power of Secretary of State to refer the matter

199. This section provides for the Secretary of State to refer the case to the CC if she believes that a special merger situation has been created, or is contemplated; a consideration specified in section 58 is relevant, and it may operate against the public interest. *Subsection (5)* provides that the Secretary of State will accept the OFT's decision as to whether a special merger situation has been created.

Sections 63 and 64: Questions to be decided on references under section 62 & Cancellation or variation of references under section 62

200. Section 63 provides that the CC will consider whether a special merger situation has been created, or is contemplated; whether – on the basis of the considerations set out in the reference – the merger may be expected to operate against the public interest; and make recommendations as to what action, if any, the Secretary of State or others should take to remedy any adverse effects.

201. Section 64 provides for the circumstances in which the CC or the Secretary of State may cancel or vary a reference.

Section 65: Investigations and reports on references under section 62

202. This section provides that the CC's report and investigation should contain its conclusions on whether a special merger situation has been created; whether it may be expected to operate against the public interest; and what actions should be taken by the Secretary of State or others to remedy these adverse effects.

Section 66: Decision and enforcement action by Secretary of State

203. This section provides that the Secretary of State must decide whether the merger may

operate against the public interest within 30 days of receiving the report from the CC and may take whatever remedial steps she considers necessary (from paragraph 9 or 11 of Schedule 7). The Secretary of State must accept the view of the CC as to whether a special merger situation has been created or is contemplated.

European Mergers

Section 67: Intervention to protect legitimate interests

204. This section allows the Secretary of State to intervene in cases where the competition issues (if any) would fall to be determined by the European Commission under the ECMR (i.e. cases other than those where competition issues are referred back for consideration under UK domestic law under Article 9 ECMR, which fall to be considered under Chapters 1 and 2 of Part 3). *Subsection (2)* provides that the Secretary of State may serve a European intervention notice if she believes that one or more than one public interest consideration may be relevant to the case. *Subsection (1)* ensures that the Secretary of State can only serve such a notice if she has a reasonable suspicion that there is or will be a relevant merger situation that is also a concentration qualifying for scrutiny under the ECMR and it is not a case (like a newspaper merger) that is specifically excluded from consideration under Chapter 1 of Part 3 .

Section 68: Scheme for protecting legitimate interests

205. This section provides for the Secretary of State to make regulations to provide for action to be taken to protect legitimate interests as permitted by Article 21(3) of the ECMR. Section 124 provides that regulations made under this power will be subject to the affirmative resolution procedure.

Other

Section 69: Newspaper mergers

206. This section provides that the general merger regime will not apply to mergers covered by the FTA 1973 newspaper merger regime, unless the Secretary of State is prevented from making a reference under that regime.

Section 70 & Schedules 6 and 9: Water mergers

207. Section 70 and Schedule 6 amend the special regime applying to mergers between water enterprises (whether water or sewerage undertakings) in England and Wales, as set out in sections 32 to 35 of the Water Industry Act 1991 (WIA 1991).

208. The current WIA 1991 provisions provide for the mandatory reference by the Secretary of State of qualifying mergers between two or more water enterprises to the CC. A qualifying merger is one where the value of the relevant water assets being taken over and those of the acquirer each exceed a specified figure (currently £30 million). Once a qualifying merger has been referred, the FTA 1973 'public interest' test is applied in a way that attaches particular weight to the principle that the ability of the Director General of Water Services ('Director') in carrying out his or her

functions under the WIA to make comparisons between water enterprises should not be prejudiced. If the CC makes an adverse finding, the Secretary of State is responsible for determining final remedies.

209. The purpose of the special water merger regime is to preserve the Director's ability to make use of 'comparative' or 'yardstick' regulation (i.e. the ability to compare the performance of different water companies for the purposes of setting robust price and customer service standards), except where there are strong wider public interest reasons for not doing so. In the absence of any significant competition in the water sector, yardstick regulation is regarded as a particularly important regulatory tool.

210. The main purpose of the changes being brought about by this section is, while retaining a special regime for mergers between water enterprises, to bring that regime more closely into line with the general merger regime whilst also ensuring that particular weight continues to be attached to the Director's ability to make comparisons between water enterprises.

211. The changes to effect a closer alignment with the general regime include:

- a switch from an assets threshold to a turnover threshold for determining whether a merger between water enterprises qualifies for a mandatory reference;

- transfer of the responsibility for making such references from the Secretary of State to the OFT;

- the transfer of responsibility for final decisions on what remedies should be applied in the event of an adverse finding from the Secretary of State to the CC; and

- in the case of a completed water merger, the time that the OFT will have to make a reference will be reduced from 6 months to 4 months from the date of the merger taking place.

212. New section 32 (duty to refer merger of water or sewerage undertaking) provides that qualifying water enterprise mergers will continue to be subject to mandatory reference to the CC, but with responsibility for making such references transferred from the Secretary of State to the OFT.

213. New section 33 (exclusion of small mergers from duty to make reference) provides that a mandatory reference shall only be made if:

- the relevant turnover of the water enterprise being taken over exceeds £10m; and

- the relevant turnover of one or more of the water enterprises belonging to the acquirer exceeds £10m.

These sums may be altered by regulations made by the Secretary of State.

214. The purpose of this provision is to exclude small mergers from the OFT's duty to make a reference. It replaces a similar provision based on asset values, but is expected to have the same practical effect as the current assets threshold of £30m in terms of the current water enterprises that will be affected. A refinement of the present statute will enable the Secretary of State to prescribe a different turnover threshold for the target and for the acquirer for the purposes of deciding whether there is to be a reference. The regulation-making powers provided in *subsections (4), (5)* and (6) of the revised section include power to make provision for the definition of relevant turnover for these purposes. The turnover will be set independently of the qualifying turnover thresholds set for the general merger regime.

215. Schedule 6 replaces section 34 WIA 1991. The new inserted Schedule 4ZA sets out the task for the CC when a water enterprise merger has been referred to it. Its first job is to determine whether a merger situation qualifying for investigation has been or will be created. If it has been or will be created, the CC has to decide whether the merger can be expected to prejudice the Director's ability in carrying out his or her functions by virtue of WIA 1991, to make comparisons between different water enterprises. Both such decisions have to be the decisions of at least two-thirds of the members of the relevant CC reporting group to be treated as valid. The Director's functions that are likely to be most relevant here and that could be prejudiced by a merger are his or her functions of setting price controls and service level targets and the related general term of reference in section 2(3)(d) of WIA 1991 to 'promote economy and efficiency on the part of water enterprises'.

216. If there is prejudice, then the CC has to decide whether to take action to remedy, mitigate or prevent the prejudice or any adverse effects that might result, and to decide what action should be taken. In deciding what action to take, the CC may have regard to the effect of any action on relevant customer benefits. The definition of a customer benefit is set out in paragraph 7. This matches the definition of customer benefits as defined for the purposes of the general merger regime.

217. Paragraph 4(1)(a) and (b) of inserted Schedule 4ZA, however, places two constraints on the circumstances in which the CC is able to have regard to customer benefits in deciding on remedies. These constraints are unique to the water regime. They provide that customer benefits can only be considered where the taking account of those benefits would not prevent a solution to the prejudice concerned, or in circumstances where the benefits are expected to be substantially more important than the prejudice concerned. These constraints are intended to ensure that the water regime continues to operate in a way that attaches particular weight to the preservation of comparator enterprises, whilst not excluding the possibility of customer benefits being taken into account if they are important enough, or if they can

be obtained in a way that does not prevent action to address the prejudice.

218.   Paragraphs 1 and 2 of inserted Schedule 4ZA provide for the general merger provisions in the Act to apply to qualifying water mergers subject to modifications contained in regulations that may be prescribed by the Secretary of State. It is envisaged that this power will be used, for example, to ensure that the general duty to remedy the effects of completed or anticipated mergers in section 41 can be adapted for the special purposes of the water regime. It may also be used to adapt the arrangements for the consideration of water mergers under the special regime to circumstances where the merger also raises a defined public interest issue.

219.   Paragraph 5 of inserted Schedule 4ZA ensures that no enforcement action will be taken against a completed merger of water enterprises if a reference was not made within 4 months of the later of: the merger taking place, or material facts about the transaction coming to the attention of the OFT or being made public. The current section provides for a six-month period. The change brings the special water regime into line with the period in the equivalent provision for the general mergers regime.

220.   Sections 32(2) and 32(3) of the current WIA 1991 set out transitional arrangements relevant when the original Act was brought into force. They are no longer required, and are therefore repealed.

221.   The amendments to sections 32–35 are concerned, as is the original Act, only with water enterprises in England and Wales.

222.   The transfer of responsibility for determining and implementing remedies under the normal mergers regime following an adverse finding from the Secretary of State to the CC requires a consequential change to section 17 WIA 1991. This section currently gives the Secretary of State a power, as part of her power to order remedies, to modify the conditions of appointment of a relevant undertaking for the purpose of giving effect to or taking account of the main remedial order. Schedule 9 revises section 17 WIA 1991 to give the power to modify conditions of appointment to the CC.

Chapter 4: Enforcement

223.   Sections 71–95 and Schedules 7 and 8 set out the enforcement powers of the OFT, CC and Secretary of State before, during and after a merger reference. As in FTA 1973, enforcement takes two forms: undertakings and orders. Undertakings are given voluntarily by one or more of the parties to a merger. Once accepted by the relevant authority, these become legally binding and enforceable in the courts. Orders are made by the authorities and prohibit the parties specified in the order from doing something or specify that they must take certain action. Before and during a reference, undertakings and orders seek to prevent any action being taken that might prejudice the eventual outcome of the merger inquiry. Following the CC's final report, an undertaking or order may be used to remedy the adverse effects on competition identified by the report. In the case of final orders, what an order can

specify is set out in Schedule 8. Under FTA 1973, orders were made by statutory instrument; the OFT and CC will now have the power to make orders on their own authority. There is a different but similar enforcement regime for those cases where the Secretary of State has intervened on public interest grounds. This is set out in Schedule 7.

Powers exercisable before references under section 22 or 33

Section 71: Initial undertakings: completed mergers

224. This section allows the OFT to accept undertakings from parties where it is considering whether to make a merger reference in relation to a completed merger. This is a new power for the OFT. It allows the OFT to act before it has reached a definite conclusion on whether to refer the merger. The OFT can ask parties to undertake not to carry out any action that might prejudice the merger reference or the ability of the CC to act following the outcome of its inquiry. These undertakings are legally-binding.

Section 72: Initial enforcement orders: completed mergers

225. This section permits the OFT to make an order where it is considering whether to make a merger reference. This is a new power for the OFT. The OFT is able to act before it has reached a definite conclusion on whether to refer a completed merger. The OFT can only make initial orders in respect of mergers that have been completed and where it has reason to believe that action is planned that could prejudice any subsequent investigation. This power is modelled on the interim order-making power in section 74 FTA 1973.

Section 73: Undertakings in lieu of references under section 22 or 33

226. This section allows the OFT to seek and accept undertakings from one or more parties to a merger in place of a reference. The purpose of accepting undertakings is to allow the OFT (where it is confident about the problem that needs to be addressed and the appropriate solution) to correct the competition problem the merger presents without recourse to a potentially time-consuming and costly investigation. This provision mirrors the existing power in section 75G FTA 1973 for the Secretary of State to accept undertakings-in-lieu, but with responsibility transferred to the OFT.

Section 74: Effect of undertakings under section 73

227. This section specifies that a reference on the same merger cannot be made if the OFT has accepted undertakings in lieu of a reference.

Section 75: Order-making power where undertakings under section 73 not fulfilled etc.

228. This section allows the OFT to make an order when an undertaking-in-lieu is not being complied with. In such circumstances, the OFT could seek to enforce the original undertaking in the courts or decide to replace it with an order. The content of such an order is limited to the matters set out in Schedule 8 (see below). This provision transfers the Secretary of State's existing powers in section 75K FTA 1973

to the OFT.

Section 76: Supplementary interim order-making power

229. This section is for use when an undertaking-in-lieu is not being fulfilled and the OFT would like to replace it with an order. It allows the OFT to act quickly to put in place an interim order while it prepares the main remedial order, including carrying out any consultation. The interim order can prevent the parties from taking any action that might prejudice the main order. This interim power is also available to the CC when they are considering replacing final undertakings with a final order.

Interim restrictions and powers

Section 77: Restrictions on certain dealings: completed mergers

230. This section applies an automatic prohibition on the parties to a completed merger, once it has been referred, to prevent them undertaking any further integration without the consent of the CC. This is a new provision, which applies only to completed mergers. It has been introduced because in almost all merger cases the authorities seek to prevent such further integration either by securing undertakings or by making an interim order.

Section 78: Restrictions on certain share dealings: anticipated mergers

231. This section applies an automatic prohibition on the parties to an anticipated merger to prevent them from acquiring any further shares in one another without the consent of the CC. This provision brings in the equivalent prohibition in section 75(4A) FTA 1973.

Section 79: Sections 77 and 78: further interpretation provisions

232. This section provides technical clarification on what constitutes an acquisition of an interest in shares for the purposes of section 78 and sets out certain common definitions for both sections.

Section 80: Interim undertakings

233. This section allows the CC to accept undertakings from one or more parties to a merger that they will not take any action that might prejudice the eventual outcome of the merger reference. This is a new provision. Section 74 FTA 1973 allowed for an interim order (see below) to be made during the course of a reference but made no provision for accepting interim undertakings. In practice, undertakings have been sought and accepted during this period, but on a non-statutory basis. This provision makes such undertakings legally-binding.

Section 81: Interim orders

234. This section allows the CC to make an order to prevent the parties to a merger from taking any action that might prejudice the eventual outcome of the merger reference. This provision is modelled on section 74 FTA 1973. It applies after a merger has been referred. An interim order can be made in respect of both completed and

anticipated mergers.

Final powers

Section 82: Final undertakings

235. This section allows the CC to accept final undertakings from the parties to remedy competition problems identified in its final report on a merger. This is based on the provisions on undertakings in section 88 FTA 1973.

Section 83: Order-making power where final undertakings not fulfilled

236. This section allows the CC to replace final undertakings with an order where the parties are not complying with the undertakings. Any order made under this section is limited to the matters set out in Schedule 8.

Section 84: Final orders

237. This section allows the CC to make an order to remedy any competition problem identified in its final report on a merger investigation. This final order may contain any of the matters set out in Schedule 8.

Schedule 8: Provision that may be contained in certain enforcement orders

238. This Schedule contains the list of matters that can be included in final orders for the purpose of remedying the adverse effects specified in the CC's report. This list is based on Schedule 8 of FTA 1973. It has been updated to reflect modern drafting conventions. Certain new remedies have also been added. These are remedies that experience has shown it would be useful to be able to call upon. The new remedies are as follows:

- paragraph 10 – the ability to require goods or services to be supplied to a particular standard or in a particular manner. This has been added to ensure that final orders can require parties to meet a certain quality of service or to continue to produce a certain range of goods. For example, it would allow an order to tell a bus company to maintain a certain frequency of service.

- paragraphs 13(3)(k) and 22 – these allow the OFT to approve the buyer of a divested business and also to approve other conduct or matters.

- paragraph 13(3)(l) – this allows for the appointment of a trustee to oversee the divestment of a business.

- paragraph 18 – the ability to specify how certain information should be published. This has been added to ensure that orders can specify that information should be published on the Internet.

- paragraph 19(c) – this allows the OFT to publish information that it is given.

- paragraph 20 – this allows for provision to be made in the interests of national security.

Public interest and special public interest cases

Section 85: Enforcement regime for public interest and special public interest cases

239. This section brings into effect the separate but similar enforcement regime for those cases when the Secretary of State has decided to intervene on public interest grounds. This regime is set out in detail in Schedule 7.

Schedule 7: Enforcement regime for public interest and special public interest cases

240. This Schedule sets out the enforcement regime that applies for cases involving a public interest consideration. The regime mirrors that of the main regime, giving the Secretary of State equivalent powers to the CC and OFT. It includes provisions for the Secretary of State to make pre-emptive orders or accept pre-emptive undertakings (paragraphs 1 and 2); these are the equivalent of initial and interim orders and undertakings. The Secretary of State may accept undertakings in place of making a reference (paragraphs 3, 4, 5). Schedule 7 includes provision equivalent to the supplementary interim order-making power set out in section 76 (paragraph 6) and the same automatic prohibitions as apply under sections 77 and 78 on further integration for completed mergers and on further share acquisition for anticipated mergers (paragraphs 7 and 8). Finally, the Schedule includes equivalent powers to accept final undertakings (paragraph 9) or make final orders (paragraph 10 and 11). Orders of the Secretary of State under Schedule 7 are made by way of statutory instrument and subject to the negative resolution procedure in Parliament (section 124(5)).

Undertakings and orders: general provisions

Section 86: Enforcement orders: general provisions

241. This section makes certain general provisions that apply to all orders.

Section 87: Delegated power of directions

242. This section allows the person making an order to give directions to an individual or to an office-holder in any company or association. Failure to comply with such directions may lead to action before the courts.

Section 88: Contents of certain enforcement orders

243. This section sets out the minimum contents of any final order or order to replace undertakings-in-lieu.

Section 89: Subject-matter of undertakings

244. This section makes clear that enforcement undertakings (which are legally enforceable) can make provision for matters that cannot be included in final orders. Thus, final undertakings differ from final orders in that the latter are limited to the

matters included in Schedule 8.

Section 90: Procedural requirements for certain undertakings and orders

245. This section gives effect to Schedule 10, which sets out the procedural requirements to be followed in making or revoking an order and in accepting or releasing an undertaking.

Schedule 10: Procedural requirements for certain enforcement undertakings and orders

246. This Schedule sets out the consultation process for making, varying or revoking certain orders or undertakings. Paragraphs 1-5 set out the process to be followed in making an order or accepting undertakings. Paragraphs 6-8 set out the process for revoking an order or releasing a party from an undertaking.

247. In both cases, the authorities will set out clearly what they are proposing to do and the reasons for it. The authorities will have to give notice of their intention to make or vary an order to the parties directly affected by it. There will be a thirty-day consultation period for orders and a fifteen-day period for undertakings, although the authorities can apply an accelerated procedure in merger cases in special circumstances (paragraph 9).

248. These procedural requirements apply to all orders and undertakings except initial and interim orders and undertakings. Initial and interim orders do not have to comply with these procedural requirements because they may need to be introduced at short notice.

Section 91: Register of undertakings and orders

249. This section creates a register to be maintained by the OFT of all orders and undertakings made or accepted by the OFT, CC or Secretary of State and of which it is aware. This register will be available to the public.

Enforcement functions of OFT

Section 92: Duty of OFT to monitor undertakings and orders

250. This section gives the OFT the lead role in monitoring undertakings and orders. The OFT will keep all undertakings and orders under review. Where it decides that an order or undertaking should be amended or revoked, it will advise the CC or Secretary of State accordingly. Where an order or undertaking is not being complied with, the OFT will be able to take the company to court. This is based on the monitoring role the DGFT currently has under section 88 FTA 1973.

Section 93: Further role of OFT in relation to undertakings and orders

251. This section allows the CC and the Secretary of State to ask the OFT to negotiate undertakings with the parties to a merger. The CC or (as the case may be) the Secretary of State retains the final say on whether undertakings should be accepted. The CC and the Secretary of State may also choose to negotiate directly with the

parties.

Other

Section 94: Rights to enforce undertakings and orders

252. This section ensures that orders and undertakings can be enforced through the courts. Any person who sustains loss or damage as a result of the contravention of an order or undertaking may bring action before the courts. The OFT may bring civil proceedings to enforce compliance with orders or undertakings. The CC and Secretary of State may also bring civil proceedings in respect of orders or undertakings for which they are responsible.

Section 95: Rights to enforce statutory restrictions

253. This section ensures that compliance with the automatic prohibitions on further integration (section 77) and on further share acquisition (section 78) can be enforced through the courts.

Chapter 5: Supplementary

Merger notices

254. This Chapter updates the merger notice procedure provided for in sections 75A-75H of FTA 1973.

Section 96: Merger notices

255. This section describes the circumstances in which a notice may be given. The section sets out that the notice should be in the form prescribed by the OFT, and that no reference will be made if the period for considering a merger notice has expired.

Sections 97 and 98: Period for considering merger notices & Section 97: supplementary

256. These sections provide for the time-periods in which a reference can be made under a notice. On receipt of a merger notice, the OFT has 20 working days, with a possibility of extending that to 30 workings days, to decide whether to refer. This reduces the FTA 1973 merger notice timetable by 5 days.

257. If an intervention notice has been served, the time-period can be extended to a maximum of 40 working days.

258. There are also circumstances in which a merger notice timetable can be extended further:

- if the parties have failed to provide information that the OFT asked for. In this case, the extension will be the period it took for the parties to provide the information;

- if the OFT is seeking undertakings. In this case the extension will be for the period it takes until undertakings are given; or up to 10 days after the OFT has received a notice saying that undertakings will not be given;

- if the European Commission is considering whether to deal with the case following a request made under article 22(3) of the ECMR;

- if the Secretary of State decides to extend her consideration of a public interest case in relation to the creation of a new public interest gateway.

Section 99: Certain functions of OFT and Secretary of State in relation to merger notices

259. This section sets out the responsibilities of the OFT in relation to merger notices. This includes: taking appropriate steps to ensure that all affected parties are made aware of the case and what the OFT should include in their notice to parties requesting information. It also provides for the circumstances in which the OFT may reject a notice. These include: if the OFT suspects that false or misleading information has been given; if they suspect that the merger will not take place; if information is not given as requested; and if the arrangements would result in a concentration with a Community dimension under the ECMR.

Section 100: Exceptions to protection given by merger notices

260. This section provides for the circumstances in which a case continues to be referable, notwithstanding the fact that the period for considering a merger notice served in that case has expired. Such circumstances include rejection of the notice by the OFT or withdrawal of it by the parties, non-disclosure of material information, and any other merger involving any relevant party.

Sections 101 and 102: Merger notices: regulations & Power to modify sections 97 to 101

261. Sections 101 and 102 provide the Secretary of State with the power to make regulations relating to the merger notice procedures and to modify sections 97 to 101.

General duties in relation to references

Section 103: Duty of expedition in relation to references

262. This section ensures that the relevant authority (either the OFT or the Secretary of State) will make its decision on reference as early as it is sensible to do so.

Section 104: Certain duties of relevant authorities to consult

263. *Subsections (1) and (2)* set out that the OFT, CC or Secretary of State will, where practicable, consult those persons who control any of the merging enterprises who are likely to be adversely affected by certain proposed decisions before those decisions are taken. *Subsection (6)* provides that this duty applies to reference decisions by the OFT and the Secretary of State and the CC's final conclusions on whether there is a substantial lessening of competition or an adverse public interest effect and on

remedies. *Subsection (3)* provides that, where practicable, those likely to be affected should be given the reasons for a proposed decision.

Information and publicity requirements

Section 105: General information duties of OFT and Commission

264. This section sets out the general duties of the OFT in relation to merger cases.

265. *Subsections (1) and (2)* ensure that the OFT will act, if practicable, to bring cases that it is investigating to the attention of those that might be affected by the transaction. This duty does not apply to merger notice cases, which carry their own publicity requirements (see note on section 99).

266. *Subsections (3) and (4)* provide that the OFT will give relevant information to the CC.

267. *Subsections (5) and (6)* ensure that the OFT and the CC will give information and assistance to the Secretary of State to enable her to carry out her functions in relation to cases that may raise public interest considerations.

Section 106: Advice and information about references under section 22 and 33

268. This section requires the OFT and the CC to publish advice and information about certain of their key tasks in the merger scrutiny process. The OFT will be required to explain how it will apply its duty to make references. The CC will have to explain how it will consider references. This information and advice will include explanations of how the OFT and CC will apply the substantive tests in the new regime, including, in particular, the application of the substantial lessening of competition test, and the circumstances and manner in which relevant customer benefits will be taken into account when the OFT considers references and when the CC is considering possible remedies. The OFT and the CC will be required to consult each other (and others they consider appropriate) in preparing their respective advice and information. It is intended that the information and advice will increase clarity for business about how the new regime works.

Section 107: Further publicity requirements

269. This section provides that the OFT, CC and the Secretary of State will publish certain decisions, most accompanied by their reasons for those decisions.

270. Where the Secretary of State decides to take enforcement action in a case raising public interest considerations, she will lay details of that decision (including reasons for it) before Parliament, as well as a copy of the relevant report of the CC.

Section 108: Defamation

271. This section protects the Secretary of State, OFT and the CC against actions for defamation as a result of their exercise of functions under the merger provisions of the Act.

Investigation powers

Sections 109–117: Investigation powers

272. Sections 109-117 set out the CC's powers to require persons to give evidence and to provide specified documents and information needed for the purposes of a merger inquiry. These sections replace the powers provided under section 85 FTA 1973. There are many similarities with the earlier investigatory powers. A key change, however, is that the CC's FTA 1973 power to initiate contempt proceedings against persons who fail to comply with notices requiring the production of documents and information and the attendance of witnesses is replaced with a power for the CC itself to impose monetary penalties for non-compliance subject to a right of appeal to the CAT. The new power to impose monetary penalties is also available to the CC when it is carrying out market investigations. In addition, it is available to the CC when it is carrying out references concerning licence modifications and other matters under various sectoral enactments such as the Airports Act 1986 and the Electricity Act 1989. The necessary amendments to these sectoral enactments are made in Schedule 25 to the Act.

273. Section 109 gives the CC a power to serve notices requiring any person to attend to give evidence to the CC or to provide it with specified documents or information by specified dates. Any notice has to set out the possible consequence of a failure to comply with the notice.

274. Section 110 sets out the enforcement powers that the CC will have. It gives the CC a power to impose monetary penalties where it considers that a person has, without reasonable excuse, failed to comply with a notice. This power replaces the current contempt sanction in section 85(7)–(8) FTA 1973: the existing provision gives the CC the power to apply to a court for a finding that a defaulter has failed without a reasonable excuse to comply with a notice; if the court does make such a finding, it can punish the defaulter as though he or she had been guilty of contempt of court.

275. The section retains a similar criminal offence to that in section 85(6) FTA 1973 for circumstances where a person intentionally alters, suppresses or destroys documents that he or she has been required to produce.

276. *Subsection (9)* provides that the CC should have regard to a statement of policy (see section 116) in deciding how to make use of the available powers.

277. Sections 111–116 set out how the power to impose a monetary penalty will operate. The CC will have discretion about whether to impose a fixed penalty or a daily rate penalty, or both. A daily rate penalty, once set, will accumulate for a period until: the requested information is provided, or the date of publication or handing over of the CC's report on the reference or, where no report is published or handed over, the latest date on which the report could have been published or handed over. The Commission may determine an earlier date at its discretion.

278. The Secretary of State will determine by order the maximum fixed and daily rate penalties that the CC will be able to impose up to the maximum of £30,000 and £15,000 respectively set out in section 111(7). Before setting or altering the maximum penalties, the Secretary of State must consult the CC and such other persons as she considers appropriate. In each case, the actual level of penalty shall be an amount that the CC considers appropriate in all the circumstances of the case. Receipts from the exercise of the power will be paid into the Consolidated Fund.

279. Parties will have a right of appeal to the CAT against decisions to impose monetary penalties allowing for a full reconsideration of the matter. A party may appeal where it is aggrieved by the imposition of the penalty, the amount of the penalty, or the date by which the penalty is required to be paid. The requirement to pay a penalty is suspended until the case is determined. The CAT may cancel or reduce (not increase) the penalty or amend the date or dates by which penalties have to be paid.

280. Section 116 requires the CC to consult on and then to publish a statement of policy in relation to the enforcement of notices under section 109. It will include the considerations that will be relevant to determining the nature and amount of any monetary penalty. These considerations will be for the CC to identify, but it is envisaged that they could include:

- the nature and gravity of the omission;

- the size and financial resources of the defaulter;

- the size of penalty that will encourage the party to co-operate;

- the scale of costs and other disbenefits that will be incurred by the CC if an inquiry has to be extended to take account of information provided late.

281. Section 117 retains the existing section 93B FTA 1973 offence for the circumstances where a person supplies false or misleading information to the CC, the OFT or the Secretary of State. The penalty for this offence is imprisonment or a fine or both.

Reports

Section 118: Excisions from reports
282. This section permits the Secretary of State to exclude information from the versions of the OFT's or CC's reports that she publishes under sections 44, 50, 61 or 65. *Subsection (4)* also provides that the body that has prepared the report will advise the Secretary of State on excisions.

Section 119: Minority reports of Commission
283. This section permits members of CC reporting groups for merger inquiries who disagree with the decisions of the majority to publish their dissenting views as part of

the report on a reference.

Miscellaneous

Section 120: Review of decisions under Part 3

284. This section allows decisions taken by the OFT, CC or Secretary of State in connection with a merger reference or possible merger reference to be reviewed by the CAT. The grounds of review are those that would be applied by a court on an application for judicial review. Case law suggests such grounds could include: (i) that an error of law was made; (ii) that there was a material procedural error, such as a material failure of an inquiry panel to comply with the Chairman's procedural rules; (iii) that a material error as to the facts has been made; and (iv) that there was some other material illegality (such as unreasonableness or lack of proportionality). Judicial review evolves over time and the approach in *subsection (6)* has been taken to ensure the grounds of review continue to mirror any such developments.

Section 121: Fees

285. This section provides that the Secretary of State may, by order, require fees to be paid to her, or the OFT for the exercise of their merger regulation functions, and those of the CC. It provides that the order may specify that fees are payable in public interest cases, special public interest cases and mergers of water and newspaper enterprises, as well as cases referred on competition grounds under sections 22 and 33. This section replaces section 152 Companies Act 1989.

Section 122: Primacy of Community law

286. This section ensures that advice or information published by the competition authorities by virtue of section 106 covers the effect of Community law where appropriate. *Subsections (3)-(5)* also ensure that a reference can be made under the domestic regime following a delay arising from the operation of the ECMR.

Section 123: Power to alter the share of supply test

287. This section provides a power for the Secretary of State to amend or replace the share of supply test set out in section 23. In exercising this power, the Secretary of State must have regard to the desirability of ensuring that any amended or new condition continues to operate by reference to the degree of commercial strength which may result from the merger. The Secretary of State must also consult the OFT and the Commission before making an order.

Section 125: Offences by bodies corporate

288. This section provides for the circumstances in which individual officers of companies, partners of Scottish partnerships and members of limited liability partnerships may be held responsible for the conduct of their companies or partnerships in committing offences. Offences may be attributable to consent and connivance, or to neglect.

Section 126: Service of documents

289. This section sets out how any document served on any person (individual, body

corporate, partnership or limited liability partnership) under the merger provisions may be served.

Section 127: Associated persons

290. This section explains, in particular for the purpose of deciding whether enterprises have come under common control or ownership, which persons will be considered to be "associated persons" under this model and therefore to be treated as one person. This includes relatives, trustees and business partners. The term "relative" is also defined in this section for further clarification. This section reflects and updates section 77 FTA 1973.

Section 128: Supply of services and market for services etc.

291. This section follows the definition of 'supply of services' in section 137(3) of the FTA 1973, with two modifications. The first modification is the inclusion of new *subsection (4)*, which provides that the supply of services includes making arrangements for a person to receive computer software or data such as information, music or photographs. This is intended to cover electronic supply. Such persons are not receiving anything in physical form and so might not otherwise be receiving 'goods'. This provision ensures that such consumers will be considered to be receiving a service. The second change is the omission from the definition of 'supply of services' of provisions corresponding to sections 137(3)(c), (d), (e) and (g) of the FTA 1973, which relate to the making of arrangements to permit the use of land in certain specified circumstances. The Secretary of State is however given a power by order to extend the definition of the supply of services involving arrangements permitting the use of land as in section 137(3A) of the FTA 1973. It is intended that this order-making power will be used to reinstate those provisions relating to the use of land in section 137(3) that are relevant to this Part before this Part of the Act comes into force.

PART 4: MARKET INVESTIGATIONS

Introduction

292. Sections 131-184 and Schedules 9 and 12 make provision for a system of market investigations to replace the existing FTA 1973 monopoly inquiries regime. The purpose of these investigations is to inquire into markets where it appears that competition has been prevented, restricted or distorted by the structure of a market (or any aspect of its structure), the conduct of persons supplying or acquiring goods or services who operate within it, or the conduct of such persons' customers, but where there has been no obvious breach of the prohibitions on anti-competitive agreements or arrangements or abuse of a dominant position under CA 1998 or Articles 81 or 82 of the EC Treaty. An example of the sort of circumstances in which these provisions might be used would be a situation where a few large firms supplied almost the whole of the market and, without there being any agreement between them (i.e. a non-collusive oligopoly), they all tended to follow parallel courses of conduct (e.g. in

relation to pricing), while new competitors faced significant barriers to entry into the market, and there was little or no evidence of vigorous competition between the existing players.

293.   As under the FTA 1973 monopolies provisions, market investigation references will be able to be made to the CC by the OFT, certain sectoral regulators, and (under a reserve power) Ministers. The CC will carry out an in-depth investigation of competition in the market or markets concerned. Where the CC identifies competition problems, their findings will be used as the basis for remedial action. The main differences between the market investigations regime and the FTA 1973 monopoly inquiries regime are as follows:

- the tests applied both by OFT and others when making a reference and by the CC when analysing markets referred to it will be focused on identifying adverse effects on the process of competition that arise from the structure of particular markets, the conduct of persons supplying or acquiring goods or services who operate within them, or the conduct of such persons' customers or suppliers (under FTA 1973 the CC's key recommendations are based on the application of a broad 'public interest' test);

- except in cases where a public interest intervention notice issued by the Secretary of State is in force (see below), the CC will be under a duty to take such steps as it considers reasonable and practicable to remedy the competition problems it identifies as a result of its investigations, together with any 'detrimental effects on customers' (in the form of higher prices, lower quality or less choice of goods or services, or less innovation in relation to goods or services in any UK market) to the extent that they arise from such problems. Under FTA 1973, any remedial action is at the discretion of the Secretary of State. The CC will have powers to accept remedial undertakings and make remedial orders similar to those that the Secretary of State has under FTA 1973;

- in considering the implications of its duty to remedy in any given case, the CC will in particular be able to take account of 'customer benefits' in the form of lower prices, greater quality or choice, or increased innovation that result from the structure or conduct from which adverse effects on competition have been found to arise;

- in certain regulated sectors (e.g. gas, electricity, water), the CC will be able (as the Secretary of State is under the monopolies regime) to exercise its powers to remedy by means of a change to certain aspects of the regulatory framework applicable to companies operating in those sectors (e.g. electricity supply licences; conditions of appointment in the water sector; and rail passenger franchise agreements and access agreements). When considering remedies in this form, the CC must take account of the statutory duties and objectives of the relevant sectoral regulator, as well as being able to take account of the standard set of customer benefits;

- the scope for consideration of any wider 'public interest' issues will be restricted to cases in respect of which the Secretary of State issues an intervention notice;

- intervention notices will only be issued in circumstances where the Secretary of State has concerns about the impact that a market investigation may have on national security or other public interest considerations that the Secretary of State believes should be specified by statutory instrument subject to the affirmative resolution procedure. There will also be a requirement to make the scope of such public interest considerations clear at an early stage in the investigation process, and provision is made for cases where an intervention notice has been issued to be considered on a 'competition-only' basis, with the CC taking the final decision, where, for example, the Secretary of State decides that a public interest consideration is not after all relevant, or fails to secure Parliamentary approval for the specification of a new public interest consideration;

- the OFT or other referring authority will no longer set a deadline for the CC to conclude its investigation. Instead, the CC will be responsible for setting its own administrative timetable in consultation with parties to the investigation, subject to a two-year statutory long-stop provision;

- the CC's proceedings will be governed by published procedural rules. It will have a power to impose financial penalties for failure, without reasonable excuse, to produce specified information.

294. Other differences and similarities between the monopolies and market investigations regimes are pointed out in relation to particular sections below.

295. References to the OFT in the explanatory notes on this Part should be construed as including relevant sectoral regulators, unless explicitly stated otherwise (see further the notes on section 136 and Part 2 of Schedule 9).

Chapter 1: Market investigation references

296. Chapter 1 (sections 131-138) sets out the substantive framework for decision-making in market investigation cases (except for those cases where the public interest intervention regime is engaged, which are covered by sections 139-153). In particular, it deals with the statutory criteria to be applied by the OFT or other referring body when making references and by the CC when investigating markets; it prescribes what the CC must cover in its report; and it sets out the CC's duty to remedy the competition problems that it identifies.

Making of references

Section 131: Power of OFT to make references

297. This section describes the criteria on which the OFT and certain sectoral regulators may make a market investigation reference. In order to make a reference, the OFT must have reasonable grounds for suspecting that one or more 'features' of a market are preventing, restricting or distorting competition in the supply or acquisition of specified goods or services.

298. *Subsection (2)* provides that, for the purposes of Part 4, the following are to be considered features of a market: (a) its structure (or any aspect of its structure); (b) the conduct of persons supplying or acquiring goods or services who operate within it; and (c) the conduct of such persons' customers.

299. The distinction between 'structure' and 'conduct' in a market is commonly made in economic analysis, and is intended to provide the framework for a wide-ranging inquiry into how firms compete in a market and the economic context in which they operate.

300. Some of the main elements that it is anticipated might be included in an analysis of market structure are outlined below:

   • *Market definition:* the starting point for an analysis of the structure of a market is market definition: the process of deciding what goods or services are included in the product market (e.g. ice creams bought from convenience outlets on the spur of the moment rather than from a supermarket) and what the geographic extent of this market is (e.g. is it local, regional, UK-wide, European, or global).

   • *Measures of market shares and concentration* can provide a rough indication of the competitive strength of those operating in a market, although they will seldom in themselves provide an unambiguous indication of market power and the state of competition in that market (e.g. the fact that three firms each have 30 per cent of a market now does not mean that the market is uncompetitive: it may be that their respective shares a year ago were quite different, or that, although their shares remain broadly stable over time, there is a great deal of customer 'churn' between them).

   • *Barriers to entry and expansion in a market:* these are factors that place actual or potential entrants into a market at a competitive disadvantage compared with established suppliers, or make it difficult for new entrants or existing smaller players to grow and thus act as an effective competitive constraint on larger incumbents. High barriers to entry and/or expansion are often a cause of competition problems in a market because they remove a competitive constraint, thus allowing the incumbents to raise prices above the competitive level, secure in the knowledge that new entrants cannot enter the market, undercut them, and win market share. Barriers to entry and expansion arise from a wide variety of causes; for example:

- laws and regulations (e.g. where only a certain number of licences is issued to operate in a market);

- sunk costs (investment costs of entering the market that cannot be recovered if the entrant subsequently exits the market) and economies of scale (which make it inefficient to operate in a particular market below a certain scale) will tend to increase the risks and difficulty of entry;

- information constraints (e.g. where it is difficult or impossible for new entrants to gain the information that they need to compete, or where it is difficult and costly for consumers to gain sufficient knowledge to switch to a new product);

- the strategic behaviour of incumbents (who may, for example, have positioned themselves so as to be able to take retaliatory action to eliminate any competitive threat posed by an entrant);

- the likelihood or rate of market growth (a growing market is more likely to be attractive to new entrants than a declining one).

- *The degree of vertical integration and vertical links:* the extent to which suppliers in a market are also active in upstream and downstream markets, or are linked with suppliers on upstream and downstream markets, may influence their competitive behaviour (as well as having an impact on the ease of entry into the market).

- *The cost or difficulty of switching from one supplier to another*: such costs can act as a disincentive to vigorous competition either between incumbents or on the part of new entrants.

- *Buyer power:* the strength of customers' bargaining position relative to that of suppliers can have a significant impact on competition in a market and on the ease of entry into it.

- *Information asymmetries:* the participants in a market will rarely all have the same information. The asymmetry of information between different participants buying or selling a product can have a significant impact on the nature and extent of competition in the market for that product. For example, in some markets consumers are poorly informed about the product in comparison with sellers (e.g. used cars); in others, sellers are poorly informed about consumers, and this may affect how they price their products (e.g. car insurance). Information asymmetries can feed in to other aspects of market structure (in particular, they may constitute a barrier to entry or a barrier to expansion, for example if information asymmetries make consumers unwilling to switch supplier). They can also play a part in the analysis of conduct where individual suppliers exploit or create informational asymmetries, for example through branding or through price discrimination (charging different prices to different customers).

301. The term 'conduct' includes any acts and omissions, whether intentional or unintentional, of the persons referred to in *subsections (2)(b) and (c)*. By the decisions they take, the way in which they make decisions, and how they respond to their rivals and potential entrants, those operating within a market can prevent, restrict or distort not only competition within that market, but also competition in the markets in which their immediate suppliers (upstream) or customers (downstream) operate, and in complementary markets (e.g. the conduct of suppliers in a market for one of a pair of complementary markets, such as printers and printer cartridges, may prevent, restrict or distort competition in the market for the other product). The conduct of consumers and other customers, as well as that of the businesses that supply them, can also affect the conditions of competition in a market, and it is therefore included in the definition of features of a market in *subsection (2)(c)*.

302. In some cases, it will be open to debate whether a given feature of a market is structural or an aspect of conduct (for example, information asymmetries and barriers to entry arising from the behaviour of incumbents could equally well belong in either category). However in indicating the range of features of a market which the competition authorities may take into account, the separate references to structure and conduct in section 131 do not require either the OFT under section 131 or the CC under section 134 to identify particular features of markets that are the subject of a reference as falling entirely within the terms of one of subsections (a), (b) or (c) to the exclusion of the others.

303. In considering whether it has reasonable grounds to suspect that features of a market are preventing, restricting or distorting competition, the OFT will have to evaluate the evidence available to it in each case. In some cases, it will be possible for a reference decision to be justified wholly or partly on the basis of indirect evidence, such as the prevailing levels of prices charged for goods or services in a market, or the prevailing levels of profitability or productivity of firms operating in that market (particularly when observed over time, or when compared to another market, in the UK or elsewhere, for similar or related products).

304. The OFT will be obliged to consult before making a reference decision, and to give reasons justifying its decision both before and after it is made (see further sections 169 and 172).

305. The power to make market investigation references is a discretionary one. The OFT is not obliged to make a reference where it has reasonable grounds for suspecting that the reference criteria are satisfied (unlike in the merger regime, where the provisions of Part 3 place it under a duty to refer in certain circumstances). Since potential market investigation cases will often raise many complex issues, the section sets no

limits to the matters that may be taken into account in deciding whether or not to make a reference, once the OFT has reasonable grounds to suspect that the reference criteria are satisfied. For example, there could be circumstances in which the reference criteria were satisfied, but the competition problems in the market concerned were of a kind that it was more appropriate for the OFT to address using its powers under CA 1998. Or the OFT might take the view that the competition problems in a market that it had the power to refer were likely only to be temporary, or were too trivial for it to be likely that the costs and burdens of a CC investigation would be justified by any likely outcome of such an investigation.

Section 132: Ministerial power to make references

306.   Under FTA 1973, the Secretary of State (acting alone or jointly with other Ministers) and the DGFT each have independent powers to make monopoly references. Certain sectoral regulators have concurrent powers of reference with the DGFT conferred by the relevant utility statutes in respect of the areas that they regulate. However, the DGFT's and sectoral regulators' powers of reference are subject to exclusions in certain sectors (in which references may only be made by Ministers) and a limited power of veto on the part of the Secretary of State. Under the market investigations regime, there will be no such limitations on the OFT's power of reference, and the Secretary of State (acting alone or jointly with other Ministers of the Crown (*subsection (5)*) retains the ability to make market investigation references only as a reserve power.

307.   *Subsections (1)-(3)* set out the circumstances in which this reserve Ministerial power of reference may be used. Like the OFT and sectoral regulators (section 130), Ministers must have reasonable grounds for suspecting that a feature or combination of features of a market are preventing, restricting or distorting competition in the supply of specified goods or services before they can make a reference (subsection (3)). However, Ministers must additionally either be dissatisfied with the OFT's decision not to make a reference (subsection (1)); or they must be satisfied that the OFT is aware of whatever evidence has led them to form a suspicion and is not likely to reach a decision as to whether or not to make a reference within a reasonable period of time (subsections (2) and (3)).

308.   *Subsection (5)* provides that references may be made by more than one Minister of the Crown acting jointly, so long as the Secretary of State is one of the Ministers making the reference.

Section 133: Contents of references

309.   This section prescribes what a reference made under section 131 or section 132 must contain and provides for the goods or services that are the subject of a reference to be described in such a way as to focus the CC's investigations on particular areas of concern that the referring authority has identified. Any authority making a market investigation reference must also publish its reasons for doing so (see further section 172).

Determination of references

Section 134: Questions to be decided on market investigation references

310. This section sets out the questions that the CC must answer in the course of conducting a market investigation under Part 4.

311. *Subsections (1)-(3):* the CC is to consider what market or markets exist in connection with the supply or acquisition of the goods or services described in the reference (the 'relevant market(s)'), and then to determine whether any feature or combination of features of the relevant market(s), prevents, restricts or distorts competition in connection with the supply or acquisition of goods or services in the UK: where this is the case, there is an 'adverse effect on competition'. Depending on the circumstances, more than one adverse effect on competition may be found (e.g. where there is more than one relevant market).

312. *Subsection (4)-(5):* where the CC identifies one or more adverse effects on competition, it must further decide what action should be taken to remedy, mitigate or prevent it or them, whether by the CC itself, or by others (including those operating in the market concerned, Ministers - who may, for example, be able to introduce changes to existing laws, so as to remove a regulatory barrier to entry - and other public authorities). The CC must also consider what action it or others should take to remedy, mitigate or prevent any 'detrimental effects on customers' (in the form of higher prices, lower quality or less choice of goods or services, or less innovation in relation to goods or services in any UK market) in so far as they have resulted from, or may be expected to result from, any adverse effect on competition that it has identified.

313. *Subsection (6):* in deciding what steps should be taken under subsection (4), the CC is to have regard to the need to achieve as comprehensive a remedy as is reasonable and practicable. Thus, all other things being equal, a remedy that, for example, removes an adverse effect on competition will be considered more comprehensive than one that only removes detrimental effects on customers resulting from that adverse effect, since by removing the adverse effect, the CC will also (at least so far as is within its power) remove the detrimental effect on customers. To that extent, there is a presumption in favour of remedial action that deals directly with adverse effects on competition over action that is directed specifically at detrimental effects on customers. The requirement to have regard to reasonableness and practicability means, *inter alia*, that the CC must, in relation to each proposed remedy, consider what effect it will have on the future conduct of those operating in the market, how it will interact with any other proposed remedies, and whether the adverse effect(s) or customer detriment(s) that it was designed to address are sufficiently serious for their removal or mitigation to justify whatever costs and disruption to businesses and others will be involved in the implementation of that remedy.

314. *Subsections (7) and (8):* in considering what steps should be taken under subsection (4) the CC may further have regard to any customer benefits (in the form of lower

prices, or higher quality or greater choice of goods or services, or greater innovation in relation to goods or services in any UK market) arising from the relevant feature or features of the market that have given rise to adverse effects on competition, provided that the benefit has accrued, or may be expected to accrue within a reasonable time, and was or is unlikely to accrue without the feature or features concerned.

Section 135: Variation of market investigation references

315. This section allows the authority that has made a market investigation reference, after consultation with the CC, to widen or narrow the scope of the CC's investigation while it is in progress. The CC itself may ask the OFT or other referring authority to vary the market investigation reference (for example, where it finds that the terms of reference are wider or narrower than are justified by its own view of the market or markets concerned, and the operation of competition within it or them). A variation will be effective immediately and any variation made to the market reference will have no impact on the statutory timetable for the investigation – i.e. the CC must still conclude their investigation within two years of the date on which the original reference was made (see further section 137).

Section 136: Investigations and reports on market investigation references

316. This section prescribes that the CC must publish a report on a market investigation reference within two years of the date on which the reference was made. *Subsection (2)* prescribes what the report must contain.

317. *Subsections (4)-(5)* provide that, as well as publishing its report, the CC must give a copy of it to the OFT and to the appropriate Minister if he made the reference. Where the reference was made by the OFT or by the appropriate Minister but could have been made by a relevant sectoral regulator the report is also to be given to them.

318. *Subsections (7) and (8)* list the sectoral regulators who have concurrent powers to make market investigation references on the same basis as the OFT in the areas that they regulate ('relevant sectoral regulators') and the provisions of 'relevant sectoral enactments' that (as amended by Part 2 of Schedule 9) confer these concurrent powers on them. Information obtained by relevant sectoral regulators in connection with the exercise of any function under this Act is protected by the information disclosure provisions in Part 9. The provisions governing concurrency between the OFT and relevant sectoral regulators, which are to be found in the sections of the relevant sectoral enactments, are essentially the same as under the FTA 1973 monopolies regime: in particular, the OFT and the relevant sectoral regulator concerned must consult each other before either makes a reference.

Section 137: Time-limits for market investigations and reports

319. This section sets out the statutory maximum period for a market investigation. Initially this is to be set at two years. A market investigation report shall be prepared and published within the statutory maximum period after the reference is made. *Subsection (3)* gives the Secretary of State a power to alter the statutory maximum by order, but not to extend it beyond two years. The making of such an order by the

Secretary of State will not affect the statutory maximum period applicable to any investigation that is the subject of a reference made before the date of the order.

Section 138: Duty to remedy adverse effects

320. This section provides that, where the CC has published its report within the statutory time-limit and has found one or more than one adverse effect on competition, it must take such action as it considers reasonable and practicable to remedy, mitigate or prevent that adverse effect and/or any detrimental effect on customers so far as it may have resulted from, or may be expected to result from, each adverse effect on competition. The duty to remedy expressed here is qualified by the same considerations (comprehensiveness, reasonableness and practicability, and discretionary consideration of customer benefits) as the analysis of remedies prescribed by section 134.

321. *Subsection (3)* provides that, unless there has been a material change of circumstances since the preparation of the CC's report, or unless it has special reason for deciding otherwise, any action taken by the CC must be consistent with the course of action decided on under section 134(4)(c), and set out in its report under section 136.

322. *Subsection (6)* provides that, where the CC has found that a detrimental effect on customers may be expected to result from a particular adverse effect on competition, but that no detrimental effect on customers has yet resulted from that adverse effect, then the CC may only take action to remedy, mitigate or prevent the detrimental effect that may be expected to arise if it remedies, mitigates or prevents the adverse effect on competition.

Chapter 2: Public interest cases

323. Chapter 2 (sections 139-153) establishes a mechanism that allows the Secretary of State to intervene in cases where she considers that her intervention is justified by wider public interest considerations. This arrangement operates independently of the Ministerial power to make references (see section 132). Where an 'intervention notice' is in force, the Secretary of State's approval is required before the acceptance of undertakings in lieu of a reference (see section 150), and the Secretary of State, rather than the CC, becomes the decision-taker on remedies after a CC investigation (see section 147). The flowchart at Annex C illustrates the procedure.

Intervention notices

Section 139: Public interest intervention by Secretary of State

324. This section provides for the Secretary of State to claim an interest in a case by serving an intervention notice on the grounds that it raises a public interest consideration. The Secretary of State is limited to raising issues that are already specified as public interest considerations in section 153 or those that the Secretary of State thinks should be specified. *Subsection (6)* ensures that, where the Secretary of State has raised any non-specified issue in an intervention notice, she will move to

specify that issue in legislation as early as practicable.

325.   *Subsection (1)* allows the Secretary of State to give an intervention notice to the CC in the first four months after a market reference is made. *Subsection (2)* allows the Secretary of State to give an intervention notice to the OFT when the OFT is considering whether to accept or to vary undertakings in lieu of a reference.

Intervention notices under section 139(1)

Section 140: Intervention notices under section 139(1)

326.   This section sets out the content requirements of an intervention notice under section 139(1) and provides when any such intervention notice will be deemed to be in force.

327.   *Subsection (1)* provides that intervention notices must include certain details, including which case they relate to, and which public interest considerations may be relevant. *Subsection (2)* gives the Secretary of State discretion to mention such public interest consideration(s) in the intervention notice as she considers appropriate where there may be more than one relevant public interest consideration.

328.   *Subsection (4)* provides that an intervention notice will come into force as soon as it is given. *Subsections (4) and (5)* provide that an intervention notice will cease to be in force once the role of the Secretary of State in relation to that case is complete (either because she has acted, including by revoking the intervention notice, or is prevented from acting in a number of circumstances set out in subsection (5)).

Section 141: Questions to be decided by Commission

329.   This section sets out the issues to be considered by the CC in a market investigation case where an intervention notice is in force.

330.   In addition to the issues that must be considered by the CC in relation to a 'competition-only' market investigation (see section 134), including the CC's preferred remedies in this context (provided for by *subsection (4)*), the CC should consider what course of action would be appropriate in the light of any eligible public interest considerations *(as required by subsection (3))*.

Section 142: Investigations and reports by Commission

331.   This section provides that the CC should conduct investigations and prepare a report on a market investigation reference where an intervention notice is in force. The report should include reasoned decisions on those issues that the CC is obliged to consider in such cases.

Section 143: Publication etc. of reports of Commission

332.   This section sets out how different types of reports should be dealt with when there is an intervention notice in force.

333.   Where the CC has concluded that there is no adverse effect on competition, or that

there is one or more than one adverse effect on competition but that no remedies should be imposed, the CC shall publish its own report. This is because there is no further role for the Secretary of State to play.

334. Where the CC has concluded that there is one or more than one adverse effect on competition and that remedies would be appropriate, the CC shall pass the report to the Secretary of State so that she may consider the impact on eligible public interest consideration(s) of the remedies to the adverse effect(s) on competition. If the Secretary of State decides that the public interest consideration(s) are relevant to the CC's preferred remedies, she will publish the report.

335. When the report is published, a copy should go to the OFT, the appropriate sectoral regulator if relevant, and – if different – the Minister that made the reference.

Section 144: Time-limits for investigations and reports: Part 4

336. This section provides that the CC must prepare its report and, depending on its decision, either publish it or give a copy to the Secretary of State within two years. Provision is made for the Secretary of State to reduce the two-year period by order (as under section 137 above). The making of such an order by the Secretary of State will not affect the statutory maximum period applicable to any investigation that is the subject of a reference made before the date of the order.

Section 145: Restrictions where public interest considerations not finalised: Part 4

337. This section provides that the CC's conclusions as set out in its report must not rely on any new public interest consideration cited in the intervention notice, unless that consideration has been approved by Parliament within a given period. This ensures that the Secretary of State is prevented from determining the outcome of a case on grounds that Parliament has not recognised.

338. The CC will be able to consider a public interest consideration cited in a relevant intervention notice only if Parliament has approved an order seeking to create such a public interest consideration, or for a period of up to 24 weeks from the date of the intervention notice. Where Parliament has not yet decided upon such an order, the CC will be prevented from giving its report to the Secretary of State for a period of 24 weeks from the date of the reference.

Section 146: Decision of Secretary of State

339. This section sets out how the Secretary of State will proceed on receipt of a report from the CC in a case raising any public interest consideration(s).

340. The Secretary of State will decide whether the CC's remedies to the adverse effect on competition would affect any eligible public interest considerations. *Subsections (3) and (4)* ensure that the Secretary of State must make and publish this decision within 90 days of receipt of the CC's report; otherwise, the report reverts to the CC

allowing it to implement its preferred remedies.

Section 147: Remedial action by Secretary of State

341.   This section sets out that, where the Secretary of State has decided that the CC's preferred approach would affect any eligible public interest considerations, she may take action to address the adverse effects on competition identified in the report concerned, with regard to what is appropriate in light of the relevant public interest considerations.

342.   *Subsection (6)* provides that, where the CC has found that a detrimental effect on customers may be expected to result from a particular adverse effect on competition, but that no detrimental effect on customers has yet resulted from that adverse effect, then the Secretary of State may only take action to remedy, mitigate or prevent the detrimental effect that may be expected to arise if she remedies, mitigates or prevents the adverse effect on competition.

Section 148: Reversion of the matter to the Commission

343.   This section sets out that the CC should act where the Secretary of State either fails to make a decision on whether public interest considerations are affected, or decides that no public interest considerations are relevant. The CC will publish its report (and give a copy to relevant bodies) and will be under a duty to implement its preferred remedies as set out in that report.

344.   Where the case has reverted to the CC to implement its preferred remedies under this section, *subsections (7)–(10)* provide that the CC must obtain the Secretary of State's agreement if it proposes to depart materially from the course of action set out in its report. However, the Secretary of State can only withhold her agreement if she believes that the CC's new proposed course of action would adversely affect the public interest. She may have regard only to the competition concerns identified by the CC and any relevant public interest considerations.

Intervention notices under section 139(2)

Section 149: Intervention notices under section 139(2)

345.   This section sets out the content requirements of an intervention notice given to the OFT under section 139(2) in relation to undertakings in lieu, and provides for when any such intervention notice will be deemed to be in force.

346.   *Subsection (1)* provides that such intervention notices must include certain details, including which case it relates to, and which public interest considerations may be relevant. *Subsection (2)* provides the Secretary of State with the discretion to mention such public interest consideration(s) in the intervention notice as she considers appropriate where there may be more than one relevant public interest consideration.

347.   *Subsection (4)* ensures that an intervention notice will come into force as soon as it is given. *Subsections (4) and (5)* provide that an intervention notice will cease to be in

force once the role of the Secretary of State in relation to that case is complete (either because she has acted, including by revoking the intervention notice, or is prevented from acting in a number of circumstances set out in subsection (5)).

Section 150: Power of veto of Secretary of State

348.   This section provides that, if an intervention notice on undertakings in lieu is in force, the Secretary of State must agree to any undertakings before the OFT accepts them. The Secretary of State can only withhold her agreement if she believes that an undertaking could adversely affect the public interest. She may have regard only to the competition concerns identified by the OFT and any relevant public interest considerations.

349.   *Subsection (5)* provides that, where new public interest consideration(s) specified in the intervention notice have not yet been approved by Parliament, the Secretary of State is prevented from giving her agreement on undertakings in lieu until either the Parliamentary procedure has run its course or 24 weeks have passed from the date of the intervention notice (whichever is the shorter).

Other

Section 151: Further interaction of intervention notices with general procedure

350.   This section ensures that, at any one time, any case is dealt with either on the 'competition-only' track or the 'public interest' track. Where a case which was subject to an intervention notice, has reverted to the 'competition-only' track because the Secretary of State has revoked the intervention notice, the statutory maximum timetable for the CC to publish its report is extended by 20 days.

Section 152: Certain duties of OFT and Commission

351.   This section ensures that the OFT and the CC pass any relevant information to the Secretary of State.

352.   *Subsection (1)* provides that the OFT will inform the Secretary of State if it believes that any case it is considering raises any issue specified in section 153 that the Secretary of State would not consider immaterial. *Subsection (2)* provides that, in the four months following a market reference, the CC will inform the Secretary of State if it believes that an investigation raises issues specified in section 153 which the Secretary of State would not consider immaterial. These provisions are intended to alert the Secretary of State to cases where she might wish to intervene on public interest grounds.

353.   *Subsection (3)* provides that the OFT and the CC must pass on to the Secretary of State any representations that they receive about the need for the Secretary of State to specify a new public interest consideration. This provision ensures that the Secretary of State is made aware of any calls for new public interest considerations to be specified in legislation.

Section 153: Specified considerations: Part 4

354.   This section lists the relevant public interest issues that may be specified by the Secretary of State in an intervention notice. *Subsection (1)* provides that 'national security' is the only consideration specified. *Subsection (3)* allows the Secretary of State, by order, to add to, remove from, or amend the considerations in this list.

Chapter 3: Enforcement

355.   Chapter 3 (sections 154-169) and Schedule 8 set out the enforcement powers of the OFT, CC and Secretary of State during and after a market investigation reference. As for the merger regime, enforcement takes two forms: undertakings and orders. Undertakings are agreements voluntarily entered into by the parties to a merger. Once agreed, these become legally-binding and enforceable in the courts. Orders are made by the authorities and prohibit the parties specified in the order from doing something or specify that they must take certain action. Under FTA 1973, orders were made by statutory instrument; the CC will now have the power to make orders on its own authority.

Undertakings and orders

Section 154: Undertakings in lieu of market investigation references

356.   This section allows the OFT to seek and accept undertakings from one or more persons in place of making a market investigation reference. This provision enables the OFT to avoid making a reference to the CC in certain cases. The OFT has to be confident it has identified an adverse effect on competition in a market in relation to which it would otherwise have made a reference. It also needs to persuade the relevant parties to agree to a course of remedial action to address the competition problem it has identified. It can then accept undertakings in lieu of making a market investigation reference. This provision mirrors the existing power in section 56A FTA 1973 for the Secretary of State to accept undertakings-in-lieu, but with responsibility transferred to the OFT.

Section 155: Undertakings in lieu: procedural requirements

357.   This section sets out the consultation process for accepting or varying an undertaking in lieu of a market reference. Undertakings-in-lieu require their own procedures because the OFT is required to set out, prior to accepting the undertaking, the terms of the market investigation reference that it would otherwise have made.

Section 156: Effect of undertakings under section 154

358.   This section specifies that where the OFT has accepted an undertaking or group of undertakings in lieu of a reference, no market investigation reference in relation to the matters in respect of which the OFT would have made a reference had it not accepted any such undertaking or group of undertakings can be made for a period of twelve months.

Section 157: Interim undertakings: Part 4

359. This section applies following the publication of the CC's report and up to the point at which the reference is finally determined. During this period the CC can accept undertakings from the parties that they will not take any action that might prejudice the eventual introduction of the final remedy following the CC's report. The Secretary of State may exercise this power in cases where there is a public interest notice in force.

360. Section 89 FTA 1973 allowed an interim order (see below) to be made during this period. No express provision was made for accepting interim undertakings. In practice, the authorities could seek and accept undertakings but these had no statutory basis.

Section 158: Interim orders: Part 4

361. This section also applies from publication of the CC's report to the point at which the final remedy is put in place. During this period, the CC can by order prevent the parties affected by a market investigation from taking any action that might prejudice the eventual introduction of the final remedy. This provision is based on section 89 FTA 1973. The Secretary of State may exercise this power in cases where a public interest notice is in force.

Section 159: Final undertakings: Part 4

362. This section allows the CC to accept final undertakings from the parties to remedy competition problems identified in its final report on a market investigation reference. This is based on the provisions on undertakings in section 88 FTA 1973. The Secretary of State may exercise this power in cases where there is a public interest notice in force.

Section 160: Order-making power where final undertakings not fulfilled: Part 4

363. This section allows the CC to replace final undertakings with an order where the parties are not complying with the undertakings. Any order made under this section is limited to the remedies set out in Schedule 8 or any closely-related remedy. (See note on Schedule 8 under Part 3 for more detail.) The Secretary of State may exercise this power in cases raising a public interest consideration.

Section 161: Final orders: Part 4

364. This section allows the CC to make an order to remedy competition problems identified in its final report on a market investigation. This final order may contain any of the remedies permitted by Schedule 8 or any closely-related remedy. The Secretary of State may exercise this power in cases where there is a public interest notice in force.

Enforcement functions of OFT

Section 162: Duty of OFT to monitor undertakings and orders: Part 4

365. This section gives the OFT the lead role in monitoring undertakings and orders. OFT will keep all undertakings and orders under review. Where it decides that an order or

undertaking should be amended or revoked, it will advise the CC or Secretary of State accordingly. Where an order or undertaking is not being complied with, OFT will be able to take the company to court. This is based on the monitoring role given to the DGFT by section 88 FTA 1973.

Section 163: Further role of OFT in relation to undertakings and orders: Part 4

366. This section allows the CC (or the Secretary of State) to ask the OFT to negotiate final undertakings on its behalf following a market investigation. The CC retains the final say on whether undertakings should be accepted. The CC may also choose to negotiate directly with the parties.

Supplementary

Section 164: Enforcement undertakings and orders under this Part: general provisions

367. This section applies certain provisions from the mergers regime (Part 3) in the context of market investigations. It also specifies the minimum contents of any order.

368. Section 86 makes certain general provisions applicable to all orders.

369. Section 87 allows the person making an order to give directions to an individual or to an office-holder in any company or association.

Section 165: Procedural requirements for certain undertakings and orders: Part 4

370. This section brings into effect procedural requirements for making, varying or revoking orders and undertakings set out in Schedule 10.

371. These procedural requirements apply to final orders and undertakings. Interim orders do not have to comply with these procedural requirements because they may need to be introduced at short notice. However, unlike in mergers, paragraph 9 of the Schedule has been excluded to ensure that undertakings and orders are published in draft in every case.

Section 166: Register of undertakings and orders: Part 4

372. This section creates a register to be maintained by the OFT of all orders and undertakings made or accepted by the OFT, relevant sectoral regulators, CC or Secretary of State. This register will be available to the public. The sectoral regulators are not required to compile and maintain such a register.

Section 167: Rights to enforce undertakings and orders under this Part

373. This section makes provision for the enforcement of undertakings and orders through the courts along the same lines as section 94 in Part 3.

Chapter 4: Supplementary

Regulated markets

Section 168: Regulated markets

374.　In regulated markets, regulators have a statutory set of objectives that go beyond preventing adverse effects on competition. These objectives are also reflected in the terms and conditions of, for example, the licences under which firms operate in such markets. Whilst the regulators have a duty to promote competition, they have other duties that go further than competition. These duties may have higher priority than the duty to promote competition (e.g. The Postal Services Commission (POSTCOMM) has an overriding duty to ensure a universal postal service). Therefore, when the CC propose remedies that involve changes to licence conditions, networking arrangements, conditions attached to permissions of airports, rail franchise agreements or access agreements or conditions of appointment in the water sector (i.e. 'relevant action'), the CC should have regard to the regulators' duties.

375.　The scheme for remedying a competition problem in a regulated market is outlined in Annex D.

Schedule 9: Certain amendments of sectoral enactments

376.　This Schedule sets out amendments to sectoral regulatory legislation. Under the FTA 1973 monopolies regime, the Secretary of State can make enforcement orders that amend licence conditions. Part 1 of the Schedule makes amendments to the sectoral enactments to extend this power to the OFT and the CC. Part 2 sets out the consequential amendments to the sectoral regulatory legislation that will be required to be made in order to give sectoral regulators the same concurrent powers in relation to the market investigations regime as they have under the FTA 1973 monopolies regime.

Consultation, information and publicity

Section 169: Certain duties of relevant authorities to consult: Part 4

377.　This section is provided to ensure that as far as is practicable the relevant authorities (the CC, the OFT and the appropriate Minister), consult with, and where practicable give reasons to, any person on whose interests they consider that a decision that they are about to make would have a substantial impact. An example of such a decision would be the OFT's decision to make a market investigation reference. This will ensure that the affected party is made aware of the authority's proposed decision and has the opportunity to make representations to the authority about this proposed decision before it is taken.

378.　*Subsection (4)* lists some of the things that the relevant authority should consider when it decides whether it is practicable to consult the party about its proposed decision and give reasons for this proposed decision. These are any restrictions that are imposed on the authority for taking action within a specific timetable, and the need to keep either the proposed decision or the reasons for this proposed decision confidential.

Section 170: General information duties

379. The purpose of this section is to ensure that in relation to market investigations, the OFT, CC and Secretary of State are able to obtain such information and assistance as they need from each other.

Section 171: Advice and information: Part 4

380. This section ensures the publication of guidance on the main aspects of the new markets investigations regime. The purpose of the guidance is to explain the relevant provisions and indicate how either the OFT or the CC expects these provisions to work, and to highlight the effect of Community law as appropriate. It is intended that guidance will increase clarity for business about how the new regime works. The duties conferred on the OFT by this section do not extend to the sectoral regulators.

381. The OFT is given a duty to prepare and publish guidance on how it will make market investigation references. This guidance can be updated or re-published at any time. The OFT is required to consult the CC and others whom it considers appropriate, for example the sectoral regulators, when publishing this guidance.

382. The CC is given a duty to prepare and publish guidance on how it will consider market investigation references. This shall include guidance on how the CC will consider customer benefits. Like the OFT's guidance, this guidance can be updated or re-published at any time, and the CC are required to consult the OFT and others whom it considers appropriate when publishing this guidance.

Section 172: Further publicity requirements: Part 4

383. *Subsections (1) to (4)* require the OFT, the CC, the Secretary of State or appropriate Minister to publish certain decisions taken under Part 4. The relevant authorities are also required to publish reasons for their decisions, although these reasons do not have to be published at the same time as the decision if this is not reasonably practicable.

384. The only exceptions to this duty to publish reasons are decisions by the OFT or the CC to inform the Secretary of State about a case raising a public interest consideration (see section 152(1) or section 152(2)).

385. *Subsection (8)* requires that the Secretary of State publish her reasons for deciding whether any public interest consideration is relevant to remedial action in a case, and for making, varying or revoking an order relating to the list of public interest considerations that allow the Secretary of State to take decisions in a case rather than the CC, although these reasons do not have to be published at the same time as the decision.

386. *Subsection (10)* provides that in a case that raises a public interest consideration, where the Secretary of State has decided to accept undertakings or make an order, or has decided to do neither of these things, the Secretary of State should lay details of

the decision, the reasons for the decision and a copy of the CC's report, before each House of Parliament.

Section 173: Defamation: Part 4

387.   This section protects the Secretary of State, other Ministers of the Crown, OFT and the CC against actions for defamation as a result of their exercise of their functions under the market investigation provisions of the Act.

Investigation powers

Section 174: Investigation powers of OFT

388.   This section provides that the OFT should have investigative powers while it is considering whether to make a market investigation reference. These powers correspond more closely to those available to the CC in market investigations, than to the powers available to the OFT before it makes a monopoly reference under section 44 FTA 1973.

Section 175: Enforcement of powers under section 174: offences

389.   This section sets out the enforcement powers that the OFT will have in relation to their general investigative powers under section 174. It provides that a person commits an offence where he or she intentionally fails to comply with a notice or he or she intentionally alters, suppresses or destroys documents that he or she has been required to produce. The punishment for either of these offences may be a fine and/or imprisonment. The section also sets out that it is an offence for a person to intentionally obstruct or delay the OFT or any person in carrying out their investigative functions under section 174 – this offence is punishable by fine only.

Section 176: Investigation powers of the Commission

390.   The investigation powers for the markets regime are described in more detail in the explanatory notes on the merger regime (see notes on merger sections 109-117). These sections set out the powers the CC will have to require persons to give evidence, and to provide specified documents and information needed for the purposes of a markets inquiry. There are close similarities with the investigatory powers currently provided under section 85 FTA 1973, but with one significant change. The CC's FTA 1973 power to initiate contempt proceedings against persons who fail to comply with notices requiring the production of documents and information, and the attendance of witnesses, is replaced with a power for the CC to impose monetary penalties for non-compliance (see notes on sections 111-116).

Reports

Section 177: Excisions from reports: Part 4

391.   This section permits the Secretary of State to exclude information from the version of the CC's report that she is under a duty to publish under section 142. *Subsection (4)* also provides that the CC will advise the Secretary of State on excisions.

Section 178: Minority reports of Commission: Part 4

392. This section permits members of CC reporting groups for market investigation references who disagree with the decisions of the majority to publish their dissenting views as part of the group's report on the reference.

Other

Section 179: Review of decisions under Part 4

393. This section makes comparable provision in relation to the review of decisions taken by public authorities under the market investigation provisions to that provided by section 120 in relation to decisions under the merger provisions.

Section 180: Offences

394. This section provides that the sections in Part 3 that deal with the provision of false or misleading information and the commission of offences by bodies corporate also apply to the market investigations regime. In the markets investigations regime, where there are references in section 117 (false or misleading information) to the Secretary of State, these also include references to the appropriate Minister as far as he or she is not the Secretary of State acting alone.

Section 182: Service of documents: Part 4

395. This section makes the same provision for the service of documents in relation to market investigation references as section 126 does in relation to merger references.

PART 5: THE COMPETITION COMMISSION

Section 185: The Commission

396. This section gives effect to Schedule 11, which amends the constitution and powers of the CC.

Section 186: Annual report of Commission

397. This section requires the Competition Commission to produce an annual report at the end of each financial year covering its activities.

Schedule 11: The Competition Commission

398. This Schedule makes various amendments to the constitution and powers of the CC. It amends Schedule 7 of CA98, which sets out the existing constitutional arrangements, in particular to add a new type of member to serve solely on the Council of the CC. The Schedule also updates the arrangements for appointing newspaper panel members so that, for example, it is the CC Chairman rather than the Secretary of State who will have responsibility for selecting individuals from the panel to serve on special newspaper merger reference groups. The Schedule also lists the effect on certain key types of decision (e.g. a decision that a merger is expected to result in a substantial lessening of competition) where the decision is not that of at

least two-thirds of the members of the group.

Section 187 & Schedule 12: Commission rules of procedure

399. This section gives the CC Chairman a new duty to make and publish rules of procedure to regulate the conduct of CC investigations under Parts 3 and 4 and the other enactments listed in paragraph 19(a)(9) of Schedule 7 to CA 1998 (as inserted by *subsection (3)*). Provision is made for the Chairman to consult with members of the CC and such other persons as he or she considers appropriate before making such rules (*subsection (4)*). The Chairman retains the existing FTA 1973 power to issue guidance to reporting groups on the conduct of references (*subsection (6)*). This may be useful for areas of procedure where some flexibility and discretion for panels is desirable.

400. Schedule 12 contains a non-exhaustive list of the matters that may be covered by the CC Chairman's rules of procedure.

PART 6: CARTEL OFFENCE

Cartel Offence

401. Sections 188-202 provide for a criminal offence for individuals who dishonestly engage in cartel agreements ('the criminal offence'). The criminal offence will operate alongside the existing regime that imposes civil sanctions on undertakings that breach the competition provisions of CA 1998. The civil regime applies to a much wider range of anti-competitive activities than are targeted by the criminal offence.

402. The proposal to introduce criminal sanctions as a deterrent to individuals engaging in cartel activity was included in the July 2001 White Paper, '*Productivity and Enterprise: A World Class Competition Regime*', and views were invited from consultees on the general concept and on a number of detailed aspects of the proposal.

403. In the light of responses to the consultation and of contacts with the authorities likely to be responsible for the new offence, the Government announced in November 2001 further details of its proposals for the introduction of the criminal offence, as follows:

- the definition of the offence to be based on individuals having dishonestly entered into horizontal agreements (i.e. agreements at the same level in the supply chain) to fix prices, share markets, limit production or rig bids;

- the investigation to be carried out by OFT investigators under a case controller from the Serious Fraud Office ('SFO'); appropriate investigatory powers to be made available to the OFT;

- the OFT to be able to issue 'no-action letters' to protect informants from prosecution;

- for investigations that lead to prosecution, the SFO to be the lead prosecutor; the OFT also to be a named prosecutor;

- the offence to be triable in either the Magistrates' Courts or the Crown Courts; the maximum penalty for the offence to be five years' imprisonment; fines to be available in addition or as an alternative.

404.   Sections 188-202 make the necessary legislative provisions to implement the criminal offence.

Section 188: Cartel offence

405.   *Subsections (1) to (6)* define the offence. They provide that an individual will be liable to criminal prosecution if he dishonestly agrees with one or more other persons that two or more undertakings will engage in one or more of the prohibited cartel activities. The offence only applies in respect of horizontal agreements (i.e. agreements relating to products or services at the same level in the supply chain). The offence is committed irrespective of whether or not the agreement reached between the individuals is implemented by the undertakings, and irrespective of whether or not they have authority to act on behalf of the undertaking at the time of the agreement.

406.   The prohibited activities are: price-fixing; limitation of production; market-sharing; and bid-rigging. These activities comprise the most serious forms of anti-competitive activity and as such are a sub-set of the practices for which undertakings may be pursued under the civil provisions of CA 1998.

407.   *Subsection (2)* specifies the four categories of prohibited cartel activity: price-fixing, limitation of production or supply, the sharing of markets, and bid-rigging. Price-fixing is defined so as to include the direct or indirect fixing of prices. Examples of indirect price-fixing would be likely to include, but would not be restricted to, agreements about relative price levels or price ranges, rebates, discounts, price-change indices, transport charges or methods of quotation. Market-sharing is defined in terms of customers so as to include the sharing of an individual customer or customers.

408.   *Subsection (3)* requires, in the case of price-fixing or limitation of production or supply, that for the offence to be committed the other party must reciprocally have intended that the agreement, if implemented according to the intentions of the parties, should result in one of these activities. This means that agreements are not criminal where the agreement only requires one party to fix prices or limit production or supply as defined. This further requirement does not apply in the case of market-sharing and bid-rigging where the activities are by definition reciprocal.

409.   *Subsections (5) and (6)* provide a definition of the activities that constitute bid-rigging for the purposes of the criminal offence. Bid-rigging is the only one of the prohibited activities where for all practical purposes the carrying out of the activity described

in this section will in itself invariably indicate a dishonest intention and amount to the commission of the offence. Arrangements of which the person requesting bids is aware are not subject to the criminal offence.

Section 189: Cartel offence: supplementary

410. This section relates to subsections 1(2)(a)-(d) and 1(3)(a)-(c) of section 183. It provides that, for agreements involving price-fixing, limitation of production and market-sharing, undertakings must be operating at the same level in the chain of supply or production. The criminal offence does not apply to so-called vertical agreements, which relate to intended activity where the two or more parties are operating at different levels in the chain of supply or production (e.g. as producer and distributor or as distributor and retailer).

Section 190: Cartel offence: penalty and prosecution

411. *Subsection (2)* sets out that the OFT and SFO will be the only named prosecutors for the offence in England, Wales and Northern Ireland. A third party could only bring a prosecution with the OFT's consent. This is designed to enable the OFT to prevent vexatious private prosecutions against recipients of leniency (see below). The Lord Advocate will prosecute the criminal offence in Scotland; no legislative provision is required.

412. The scope of the offence generally extends to agreements that are implemented or intended to be implemented in the UK. This means that in general agreements do not need to have been implemented for an offence to have been committed. *Subsection (3)* provides for the exception to this, which is that agreements reached overseas may only be prosecuted if some subsequent action is taken within the UK to further the agreement. An instruction to others to implement the agreement, delivered into the UK by telephone or electronic mail, might be a sufficient action for this purpose.

413. *Subsection (4)* provides for the leniency process. It provides the OFT with the power to issue an applicant for leniency with a written notice that he or she will not be prosecuted for the particular matter under investigation provided certain contractual conditions set out in the notice are met. These conditions would be likely to include that the applicant: makes an admission of guilt; must not be the lead cartel member; must cease all involvement in the cartel (except as directed by the OFT to avoid arousing the suspicions of the other parties); must co-operate fully with the investigation; and must make a full disclosure. The notice is intended to encourage informants to come forward by providing them with sufficient comfort that they will not be prosecuted. In Scotland, the decision to prosecute rests with the Lord Advocate, who will take into account a report from the OFT.

Section 191: Extradition

414. This section provides that the criminal offence, or a conspiracy or an attempt to commit it, shall be an extraditable offence to which Schedule 1 to the Extradition Act 1989 applies. That Schedule preserves the old extradition regime under the Extradition Act 1870. This will allow extradition in respect of the offence from the

UK to countries with whom the UK signed bilateral extradition treaties before 1989 – this group includes the United States of America. Requests for extradition to other countries with whom the UK has extradition arrangements (including members of the Council of Europe, Commonwealth countries and Hong Kong, and countries with whom the UK signed bilateral treaties since 1989) are considered under the main provisions of the Extradition Act 1989. Extradition from the UK to these countries will apply in respect of the criminal offence without a specific legislative provision. The extradition provisions do not apply retrospectively.

415.   Dual-criminality applies (i.e. a request for extradition may only ever be made to a country that has criminal penalties for the same activity). Thus the introduction of criminal penalties in the UK will make it possible for other countries that criminalise the same activity to request the extradition of individuals from the UK. Requests made by the UK for the extradition of individuals from other countries will be governed by the law of those countries.

Criminal investigations by OFT

416.   Sections 192-202 make provisions for appropriate powers of investigations in respect of the criminal offence. They provide the OFT with powers modelled broadly on those already available to the SFO under Section 2 of the Criminal Justice Act 1987 ('CJA87'). The OFT will investigate the criminal offence under the powers provided in these sections, working closely with the SFO, who may draw on their CJA87 powers.

Section 192: Investigation of offences under section 188
417.   This section provides that the OFT is only to exercise the powers in sections 193 and 194 in relation to the criminal offence. The OFT will continue to conduct investigations in relation to infringement of Chapter I civil prohibitions of CA 1998 by using investigatory powers set out in Part I, Chapter III of CA 1998. The OFT can only exercise the powers if there are reasonable grounds for suspecting an offence under section 188.

Section 193: Powers when conducting an investigation
418.   *Subsection (1)* provides powers for the OFT to require in writing the person under investigation, or any other person, to answer questions or provide information that the OFT considers relates to any matter relevant to the investigation.

419.   *Subsection (2)* provides that the OFT may require the production of documents that appear to the OFT to relate to the investigation. The documents required must be specified or described in a written notice or must fall within a category specified or described in the notice.

Section 194: Power to enter premises under a warrant
420.   This section makes provision for the OFT to make an application to a judge of the High Court, or in Scotland for the procurators fiscal to apply to the sheriff court, for a

warrant authorising a named officer of the OFT to enter premises. The warrant may also cover any other person whom the OFT has authorised in writing to accompany the named officer. This section parallels section 28 CA 1998, which requires the OFT to seek a warrant from the High Court or the Court of Session in order to investigate infringements of the civil prohibitions in Chapter I of CA 1998.

421. *Subsection (1)* grants a judge of the High Court or a sheriff the power to issue a warrant if he or she is satisfied that there are reasonable grounds for believing there are documents on any premises that the OFT has the right to require under section 193. The judge or the sheriff must be satisfied that one of the following circumstances applies before he or she may issue a warrant: (i) that a person has failed to comply with a requirement under section 193 to produce documents; (ii) that it is not practicable to serve a notice under section 193; or (iii) that the service of such a notice might seriously prejudice the investigation (i.e. there are reasonable grounds to believe that information might be destroyed or tampered with).

422. *Subsection (4)* allows people who are not employees of the OFT to accompany and assist OFT officers who are exercising powers under this section. It is anticipated that such people will have expertise that is not available within the OFT but is required to exploit fully the terms of the warrant (e.g. IT experts).

423. *Subsection (6)* amends Part I of Schedule 1 of the Criminal Justice and Police Act 2001 ('CJPA 2001') to add to it the powers of seizure conferred by subsection (2). This will have the effect of incorporating the amendments to statutory powers of seizure introduced by section 50 CJPA 2001.

424. These amendments enable an officer to seize material if it is not reasonably practicable to determine on the premises whether the material is seizeable or not, or, in the case of property some of which is seizeable, which items he or she would be entitled to seize. The exercise of the powers is subject to strict safeguards, which include a requirement to give written notice (section 52 CJPA 2001) and a duty to return legally privileged material (section 55).

425. The OFT's existing civil powers of seizure under section 28(2) CA 1998 are already contained in Part I of Schedule 1 of the CJPA 2001.

Section 195: Exercise of powers by authorised person

426. This section grants the OFT the power to authorise any competent investigator who is not an officer of the OFT to exercise the powers conferred on the OFT under sections 193 and 194. However, no person under investigation is bound to comply unless such authorised person produces evidence of his or her authority.

Section 196: Privileged information etc.

427. This section requires legal professional privilege - i.e. the principle that legal advice is confidential to the client to whom it is given - to be respected in the exercise of powers under sections 193 and 194 and reproduces the requirements in respect of

banking professional privilege in section 2(10) CJA 1987.

Section 197: Restriction on use of statements in court

428. This section provides that statements made under compulsion in response to powers exercised under sections 193 and 194 may only be used in court in respect of a prosecution of the person who made them: (i) for making false or misleading statements under subsection 201(2); or (ii) for making an inconsistent statement in respect of a prosecution for another offence.

Section 198: Use of statements obtained under Competition Act 1998

429. The Chairman of the OFT ("the Chairman") will continue to have the powers of the former DGFT to require the provision of information by an individual on behalf of an undertaking under Part I, Chapter III of CA 1998 as part of a civil investigation. This section amends CA 1998 to provide a safeguard with regard to the use of any such oral information obtained under CA 1998 by compulsion, for the purpose of the criminal offence under section 188. This is intended to provide protection against self-incrimination.

Section 199 & Schedule 26: Surveillance powers & Repeals and revocations

430. Section 199 and Schedule 26 amend the Regulation of Investigatory Powers Act 2000 ('RIPA 2000') to grant the OFT access to intrusive surveillance powers for the United Kingdom. With these powers the Chairman may issue an authorisation for the planting of surveillance devices in residential premises (including hotel accommodation) and private vehicles. (A designated officer may grant an authorisation in an urgent case if the Chairman is not available.) Acting on information received from an informant, the OFT could, for example, use these powers to record a meeting of cartelists in a hotel room.

431. Under section 32(3)(b) RIPA 2000, one of the criteria for which an authorisation may be granted is for 'the purpose of preventing or detecting serious crime'. All applications for authorisations are subject to the scrutiny and approval of the surveillance commissioners in line with the existing procedural safeguards in RIPA 2000. When an authorisation is granted, the OFT intends to outsource the technical deployment of the intrusive surveillance activity to other public authorities which already have access to these powers and practical experience of exercising them.

432. The OFT has applied separately to the Home Office for an Order to grant authorised officers access to directed surveillance (essentially monitoring the movement of people and vehicles) and covert human intelligence sources (essentially the use of informants) under sections 28 & 29 RIPA 2000. OFT has also applied to the Home Office for an Order to grant authorised officers access to communication data (primarily postal and telephone records) under section 22 RIPA 2000. These powers will be available for both civil and criminal investigations.

Section 200: Authorisation of action in respect of property

433. This section amends Part III of the Police Act 1997 to grant the Chairman and a

designated officer the powers to issue authorisations to interfere with private property. Such authorisations are required to gain access to premises in order to undertake intrusive surveillance.

Section 201: Offences

434.   This section makes it an offence for a person to fail to comply with any requirement imposed on him or her in an investigation by the OFT under sections 193 and 194. It is an offence for a person knowingly or recklessly to provide false or misleading information to the OFT or for a person to destroy or falsify documents that he or she has been required to produce. It is also an offence for a person to obstruct a person exercising powers under a warrant issued under section 194.

PART 7: MISCELLANEOUS COMPETITION PROVISIONS

Powers of entry under 1998 Act

Section 203: Powers of entry

435.   This section amends sections 28, 62 and 63 CA 1998 to allow people who are not employees of the OFT to accompany and assist OFT officers on raids conducted under the auspices of a warrant. It is anticipated that such people will have expertise that is not available within the OFT but is required to fully exploit the terms of the warrant (e.g. IT experts).

Directors disqualification

Section 204: Disqualification

436.   A person who is subject to a disqualification order made under the Company Directors Disqualification Act 1986 ('CDDA 1986') may not:

- be a director of a company;

- act as a receiver of a company's property; or

- in any way, whether directly or indirectly, be concerned or take part in the promotion, formation or management of a company;

without the leave of the court; or

- act as an insolvency practitioner;

for the period specified in the order. It is a criminal offence to contravene a disqualification order. Civil liabilities may also be incurred in respect of such contravention.

437. This section inserts five new sections into CDDA 1986 to enable the courts to protect the public by disqualifying a person in consequence of his or her involvement in an infringement of competition law.

438. New section 9A provides that the court must make a disqualification order against a person for a period of up to 15 years if two conditions have been satisfied. The first condition is that the person is a director of a company that has committed a breach of competition law. This is defined as an infringement of either the prohibitions in CA 1998 or the EC Treaty relating to agreements preventing, restricting, or distorting competition or abuse of a dominant position. The second condition is that the court considers the person's conduct was such as to make him unfit to be concerned in the management or control of a company. Applications for a disqualification order may be made by either the OFT or a specified regulator.

439. New section 9B provides that a person whom the OFT or regulator considers unfit may consent to a period of disqualification without the need for court involvement by giving a disqualification undertaking to the OFT or regulator. The maximum period of disqualification is 15 years.

440. New section 9C provides the OFT and regulators with powers of investigation to enable them to decide whether to make a disqualification application. These powers are the same as those that are available for an investigation into a suspected infringement of CA 1998. It also provides that, before it can make a disqualification application, the OFT or regulator must give prior notice to the person likely to be affected by the application, and give him or her the opportunity to make representations.

Miscellaneous

Section 205: Super-complaints to regulators other than OFT

441. This section empowers the Secretary of State to impose super-complaint duties on any of the sectoral regulators able concurrently to exercise powers under CA 1998, in connection with super-complaints made to them relating to their sectors (see also section 11). The Secretary of State will be able to amend the list of regulators specified where necessary thereafter.

Section 206: Power to modify Schedule 8

442. This section allows the Secretary of State to amend or add to the list of remedies that can be used in final orders. This new provision is intended to allow the list to evolve over time in response to market developments.

Section 207: Repeal of Schedule 4 to the 1998 Act

443. *Subsection (1)* removes section 3(1)(d) of and Schedule 4 to CA 1998. These provisions create a special regime dis-applying the Chapter I prohibition to the professional rules of those bodies listed in Part II of Schedule 4 and that have applied

for designation of their rules under the Act.

Section 208: Repeal of Part 6 of Fair Trading Act 1973

444.   This section repeals sections 78 to 80 FTA 1973, which made provision for Ministers to make general references and restrictive labour practice references to the CC.

Section 209: Reform of Community competition law

445.   Since the reforms made by CA 1998, a major part of the regulation of competition in the UK is modelled on the EC competition rules. Thus the prohibitions in Articles 81 and 82 of the Treaty correspond to the 'Chapter I' and 'Chapter II' prohibitions in CA 1998, and many of the powers of the OFT under that Act correspond to the powers of the European Commission contained in the EC implementing legislation made under Article 83 of the Treaty.

446.   The European Commission has made a proposal for a Council Regulation under Article 83 that would substantially revise the way EC competition law is enforced (the 'Modernisation' regulation). This proposal is currently under discussion in the EU Council.

447.   If adopted by the Council, the Modernisation regulation would give national competition authorities and courts a much greater role in the enforcement of Articles 81 and 82, and would also transform the way in which the exception provided by Article 81(3) is applied. Under the current system (the 'notification system'), agreements may be notified to the Commission in order to obtain an individual exemption granted under Article 81(3), and agreements or conduct may be notified in order to obtain a decision that the agreement or conduct does not infringe Article 81(1) or Article 82. Under the new system, such procedures would be abolished. Instead, Article 81 in its entirety would be applied directly by national courts and authorities (as well as by the Commission), and businesses would no longer be able to apply to the Commission to obtain such exemptions or decisions.

448.   Although some provisions of the regulation would be directly applicable in UK law, others would require further implementation to be given effect. Measures that are required in order to give effect to the EC provisions (e.g. by setting out the powers of the OFT in applying Articles 81 and 82) can be made under the powers given by the European Communities Act 1972.

449.   If, however, it is judged desirable to keep UK competition law in step with the EC system, as so reformed, it will be necessary to make appropriate changes to the UK system, and in particular to CA 1998. The powers provided by this section are designed to enable the appropriate amendments to be made. Thus the Secretary of State will have the power to eliminate or reduce any differences that would result from Modernisation, or from any subsequent further changes to EC competition law following a regulation or a directive made under Article 83 of the Treaty.

450. The following are examples of how the power may be used:

   • to ensure that the Chapter I prohibition does not apply to an agreement that satisfies the conditions in section 9 CA 1998 (the criteria for individual and block exemptions), without any need for a decision by the OFT to that effect;

   • to remove the process whereby parties to an agreement, or authors of conduct, may notify the agreement or conduct to the OFT for guidance or a decision as to whether it is caught by the relevant prohibition;

   • to specify the decisions that the OFT may take following an investigation. At present the powers to take decisions in relation, in particular, to the inapplicability of the Chapter I or Chapter II prohibitions are set out in detail in provisions that relate to applications under the notification system; it may therefore be necessary to set them out in similar detail, but in the context of the new system.

451. *Subsection (1)* sets out the basic power to modify CA 1998. The modifications that can be made are those considered appropriate in order to eliminate or reduce such differences between UK competition law (as contained in CA 1998) and EC competition law as may result from the making of a relevant Community instrument. The power may also be used to avert the creation of such differences, by ensuring that the appropriate changes to UK competition law move in synchrony with the changes to the EC system.

452. *Subsection (2)* defines expressions used in *subsection (1)*, in particular those which provide the basis of the comparison that must be made in exercising the power under that subsection. Thus the differences that may be dealt with under *subsection (1)* are those between the 'domestic provisions' of the CA 1998, on the one hand, and EC competition law, on the other. For those purposes, EC competition law will include not only, for example, the directly applicable provisions of a Council regulation, but also any provisions of UK law that implement or give effect to the EC competition rules. Conversely, 'domestic provisions' of the CA 1998 will exclude any measures implementing or giving effect to the EC rules. When an instrument is made under Article 83 of the Treaty and implemented in UK law (for instance using the powers given by section 2(2) of the European Communities Act 1972), it is clear that a difference may then arise, in particular, between domestic provisions of the CA 1998 previously modelled on the EC competition rules, and those rules as amended in consequence of the new Community instrument. In those circumstances, the power in *subsection (1)* may be used in order to reduce or eliminate such differences.

453. *Subsection (3)* provides a separate power to repeal or modify any provision of an Act (other than the 1998 Act) which excludes any matter from the prohibitions in the 1998 Act. Examples of such statutes are paragraph 9 of Schedule 14 to the Companies Act 1989 (agreements relating to bodies which are recognised regulatory or supervisory bodies under that Act) and sections 164, 311 and 312 of the Financial Services and

Markets Act 2000 (various agreements and conduct within the scope of that Act).

454. *Subsections (4) to (8)* make further provision as to the relevant powers, including provision permitting the powers to be used to sub-delegate the power to make subordinate legislation and provision removing the restriction in the European Communities Act 1972 in relation to regulations implementing a Community instrument to which this section applies. The affirmative resolution procedure applies to any use of the powers given by this section.

PART 8: ENFORCEMENT OF CERTAIN CONSUMER LEGISLATION

Introduction

455. This Part of the Act is intended to strengthen consumer protection by giving enforcement bodies wider powers to obtain court orders (similar to injunctions) against businesses which do not comply with their legal obligations to consumers. It will replace Part III of FTA 1973 and the Stop Now Orders (EC Directive) Regulations 2001 ('the SNORs').

456. Part III of FTA 1973 was intended to provide a means of dealing with traders who, ignoring the constraints imposed by civil or criminal law, operate their business in a way that is detrimental to the interests of consumers. Under FTA 1973 the DGFT can apply for an order that the trader refrain from continuing a course of conduct that is unlawful and detrimental to consumers.

457. Three principal defects have been identified with the Part III enforcement regime.

458. First, most traders whose behaviour raises concerns for the purposes of Part III operate at local level. Consumer protection legislation is largely enforced by weights and measures authorities (trading standards departments), but under Part III of FTA 1973 they have to refer cases suitable for action to the DGFT.

459. Second, the DGFT can only apply for a court order if, after using his best endeavours, he has been unable to obtain a satisfactory written assurance from the trader in question that he will refrain from continuing that course of conduct or a similar one, or that such an assurance has been broken. This has given traders scope for delay by entering into lengthy discussion about the terms of the assurance.

460. Third, the OFT has reported that the courts, in considering applications for Part III orders, require evidence of a large number of instances of unlawful conduct before they will find that a person has 'persisted in a course of conduct'.

461. The 1999 Consumer White Paper *'Modern Markets: Confident Consumers'* included a commitment to legislate to rectify the principal weaknesses in the Part III

enforcement regime.

462. Partial reform of Part III has already taken place through the SNORs, which implement Directive 98/27/EC of the European Parliament and of the Council of 19 May 1998 on injunctions for the protection of consumers' interests (known as the 'Injunctions Directive'). The purpose of the Injunctions Directive is similar to that of Part III: it permits consumer protection bodies ('qualified entities') designated by the Member States to apply to the courts or competent administrative authorities for orders to require traders to cease conduct that constitutes a breach of any of the consumer protection directives listed in the annex to the Injunctions Directive and that harm the collective interests of consumers. Qualified entities can bring proceedings in their own Member State and in another Member State if an infringement there has effects on consumers in the qualified entity's home State.

463. The Injunctions Directive was added to the European Economic Area Agreement by Decision No 121/1999 of the EEA Joint Committee, which came into force on 1 July 2000.

464. The effect of the SNORs was to replace the grounds for an order under Part III with that required by the Injunctions Directive and to correct other perceived defects with the Part III process, in so far as Part III applies to the UK legislation implementing the specified consumer protection directives. The SNORs:

- extended enforcement jurisdiction to trading standards departments and other designated bodies;

- limited the time during which voluntary compliance must be sought to two weeks; and

- replaced the 'persisted in a course of conduct' test with a requirement that the enforcement authority demonstrate that the trader has engaged, or is likely to engage, in conduct that constitutes an infringement of one of the specified directives as transposed in the UK, where the infringement harms the collective interests of consumers.

465. The result has been the creation of two separate enforcement regimes aimed at rectifying similar conduct by similar offenders. The SNORs, which were made under section 2(2) of the European Communities Act 1972, could not have dealt with the perceived defects in Part III in respect of unlawful conduct detrimental to consumers outside the scope of the Injunctions Directive.

466. When brought into force, this Part of the Act will create a single, unified enforcement regime across the consumer field. The remedies to be available to enforcing bodies and the procedures to obtain them are based on those presently provided for in the SNORs. However, this Part will also enable a court order to be made to secure enforcement of domestic law requirements not covered by the SNORs but currently

available under Part III of FTA 1973 only to the DGFT ('domestic infringements').

467. If requested to do so by the DGFT, the statutory regulators for the gas, electricity, water, rail, and telecommunications industries have the power to make applications under Part III within the fields they regulate. All of these statutory regulators are qualified to bring proceedings under the SNORs, and it is proposed to designate them as enforcers under this Part.

Section 210: Consumers

468. This section defines the class of consumers who are to benefit from the protection provided for in this Part. A distinction is made between a 'consumer' for the purposes of a 'domestic infringement' and a 'consumer' for the purposes of an infringement of the legislation to which the Injunctions Directive applies (a 'Community infringement').

469. A 'consumer' in relation to a domestic infringement is an individual who receives, or seeks to receive, goods or services other than in the course of his business, or with a view to setting up a business, from a person who supplies them in the course of business (*subsections (2) to (4)*). The definition of a consumer for the purposes of domestic infringements therefore excludes partnerships and corporate bodies.

470. The purpose of including prospective business people within the above definition of 'consumer' is to ensure that an enforcement order is available in respect of domestic infringements that harm the collective interests of individuals who participate in, for example, 'homeworking schemes' or who contract with so-called 'vanity publishers' or who purchase goods and services for the purpose of direct selling type schemes. As soon as an individual begins trading he will cease to be within the definition in respect of purchases for the purpose of his business, so business customers in general are not covered.

471. For the purpose of domestic infringements, it does not matter if the supplier has a place of business in the UK or not (*subsection (5)*). This means businesses will not be able to avoid the provisions of this Part by locating offshore.

472. The concept of "business" is relevant to the definition of a "consumer" for the purposes of a domestic infringement in two ways. The supply, actual or attempted, of goods or services must be "in the course of a business carried on" by the supplier, but the recipient must not receive them "in the course of a business carried on by him" at the time of receipt.

473. *Subsection (8)* defines a 'business' for the purpose of the definition of the supplier of goods and services and of a consumer in respect of domestic infringements. Any undertaking carried on 'for gain or reward' and any which charges for the supply of goods or services are businesses within the definition. This follows the existing definition in FTA 1973.

474.   For the purposes of Community infringements, 'consumers' must include all persons who are consumers for the purposes of the individual directives listed in the annex to the Injunctions Directive; otherwise the Injunctions Directive would not be properly implemented. *Subsection (6)* accordingly provides that the meaning of 'consumer' in relation to a Community infringement is to be determined by the Injunctions Directive and the relevant listed directives.

475.   There is no reference in the Injunctions Directive to infringements having been committed by a person in the course of business, or any similar limitation. Although the directives listed in the annex to the Injunctions Directive mainly require Member States to impose obligations on persons carrying on business in the general sense, the identification and definition of those persons vary considerably. For this reason there is no express requirement in this section that persons only engage in conduct constituting a Community infringement if they do so in the course of business.

476.   Schedule 13 lists the individual directives, or parts of individual directives, to which the Injunctions Directive applies (*subsection (7)*). *Subsection (9)* provides the Secretary of State with an order-making power to modify Schedule 13 by adding or removing directives to reflect further amendments to the Injunctions Directive.

Sections 211 and 212: Domestic infringements & Community infringements

477.   These sections set out the types of detrimental conduct in respect of which an enforcement order under this Part can be made.

478.   Because the intention is that this Part should replace the SNORs while continuing to fully implement the requirements of the Injunctions Directive, the starting point for the scope of this new enforcement regime is the infringements to which the Injunctions Directive applies. The Injunctions Directive applies to any act contrary to the directives listed in the annex thereto as transposed into the internal legal order of an EEA State that harms the collective interests of consumers (Article 1.2). It also applies to breaches of national provisions that go beyond the minimum level of the listed directives as permitted by those directives (see below).

479.   The listed directives (or parts of them) contain a wide range of consumer protection measures, including those on unfair contract terms, misleading advertising, doorstep and distance selling, electronic commerce, and the sale of consumer goods, as well as directives dealing with particular sectors such as package travel, consumer credit, timeshare and medicines advertising.

480.   The Injunctions Directive does not affect the rules as to the applicable law in cross-border cases (see Article 2.2). It would not, for this reason, be sufficient for this Part to apply only to UK law transposing the listed directives because the Injunctions Directive would not then be properly implemented. This Part must be capable of providing for the situation where a UK court decides that the law of another EEA State should apply. This could happen where a trader's unlawful conduct in the UK harms consumers in another EEA State. In most cases, the laws of the EEA States

will be the same for the purpose of these cases, because they will all give effect to the listed directives. In most cases, it is only where an EEA State's legislation provides greater protection for consumers as allowed for under the 'minimum clause' contained in most of the listed directives that there may be a significant difference in the outcome, depending upon which State's law the court decides to apply.

Section 212: Community Infringements

481. *Subsections (1) and (2)* of section 212 provide a definition of a Community infringement that is in accordance with Article 1(2) of the Injunctions Directive. The definition refers to 'acts or omissions' that contravene provisions of listed directives as transposed by an EEA State. The concept of an omission is implicit in the Injunctions Directive because for some of the individual directives a contravention will arise (and in some cases will only arise) because of an omission. Schedule 13 lists the individual directives, or parts of individual directives, to which the Injunctions Directive, and therefore the definition of a Community infringement, applies (section 212(4)).

482. Section 212(3) provides the Secretary of State with an order-making power to specify, for the purpose of the definition of a Community infringement, the UK laws that give effect to the listed directives or that provide 'additional permitted protections'.

483. 'Additional permitted protections' are provisions that have been adopted or retained by an EEA State pursuant to the so-called 'minimum clause' contained in most of the directives (section 212(2)). These clauses enable EEA States to adopt or retain provisions that provide greater protection for consumers, on matters within the scope of the directive concerned, provided the protection does not breach the rules in the EU Treaty on, for example, the free movement of goods. A simple example would be where a directive provides for a cooling-off period, say seven days, during which a consumer may cancel the contract without penalty but an EEA State's law provides a longer period, say ten days. In contrast, a measure that provides a type of protection that is outside the scope of a listed directive is not an 'additional permitted protection' because it cannot be said to rely on the minimum clause in the directive: the provision would not be within the scope of the directive and the infringement would not therefore fall within the Injunctions Directive. For example, the Consumer Credit Act 1974, which implements the Consumer Credit Directive, also regulates consumer hire agreements which are not dealt with in the directive at all. Breaches of the provisions on consumer hire will not therefore be Community infringements. But it is sometimes difficult to distinguish between national measures that rely on a minimum clause in a directive and measures that are not within the scope of a directive.

484. The power in section 212(3) will be used to specify the legislation that gives effect in UK law to the listed directives. This will be helpful to enforcers and the courts in dealing with cases.

485. For a Community infringement to have occurred it is not sufficient that there has been an act or omission contrary to one of the listed directives (including additional

permitted protections in the EEA State concerned). The act must also 'harm the collective interests of consumers'. The Injunctions Directive does not define the 'collective interests of consumers'. But the term (already used in the SNORs) is used in the Act in defining Community infringements so as to be sure that the UK continues to fully implement the requirements of the Injunctions Directive. For consistency, the same test has been applied for domestic infringements.

486. For both Community and domestic infringements, the Department does not consider that harming the collective interests of consumers means that a large number of consumers must already have been harmed. The Department believes it simply means that a continuation or repetition of an act or omission specified as a Community or domestic infringement could harm the collective interests of consumers, since the interests of future customers of the trader are actually or will potentially be affected. For example, if a trader has not complied with the requirement to inform consumers of their rights to cancel under the Consumer Protection (Distance Selling) Regulations 2000 when they purchase by mail order, the Department would expect the court to find it would be harmful to the collective interests of consumers for the trader to repeat the omission.

487. Similarly, the Department considers that the "harm to the collective interests of consumers" test would be satisfied where an unlawful practice is employed in relation only to goods or services purchased by a very small minority of the community (eg expensive luxury goods) and the general mass of consumers are therefore unaffected.

488. The Department considers that the phrase 'collective interests of consumers' in the Injunctions Directive (and in the Act) is intended to produce the consequence that the procedure is not available to provide redress for individual consumers who may have been harmed by an infringement.

Section 211: Domestic Infringements
489. In addition to Community infringements this Part also applies to domestic infringements as defined in section 211. The definition of a domestic infringement consists of three elements: an act or omission must be done by a person in the course of business; it must fall within section 211(2); and it must harm the collective interests of consumers in the UK. The 'harm test' is the same as that for Community infringements described above.

490. *Subsection (2)*, which provides the second element of the definition, gives the Secretary of State the power to specify by order the acts and omissions consisting of breaches of legislation or common law, as set out in section 211(2)(a)-(g), for the purposes of the definition of a domestic infringement. The legislation to which this provision applies includes Northern Ireland legislation.

491. Section 211(2)(a) enables the order to specify acts or omissions which consist of a contravention of an enactment that imposes a duty, prohibition or restriction enforceable by criminal proceedings. It is immaterial whether the duty, prohibition or

restriction is imposed in relation to consumers or not, so that, for example, breaches of legislation that serve equally to protect businesses as well as consumers will qualify (section 211(4)(a)). It is not necessary for a person to have been convicted of any offence in respect of the act or omission (section 211(4)(d)).

492.   Section 211(2)(b) and (c) enables an order to specify things done, or omitted to be done, in breach of contract or in breach of a non-contractual duty (for example, a statutory duty or a duty under the common law of negligence). It is immaterial whether civil proceedings in respect of the breach of contract or breach of duty have been brought or not (section 211(4)(c)). It is also to be immaterial whether or not that breach is waived by the consumer (section 211(4)(e)). For example, the consumer may decide to keep goods despite the fact that they were not supplied in the condition required by the contract. Another example would be where a consumer agrees to waive a breach of a contractual term such as a clause in a car hire agreement that the vehicle will have air conditioning.

493.   *Subsection (2)(a)-(c)* reflects the existing scope of Part III of the FTA 1973. Section 211(2)(d) enables the order to specify as within the definition of a domestic infringement acts or omissions for which legislation provides a remedy or sanction enforceable in civil proceedings, although no duty is expressly placed on a person not to engage in such conduct. It is immaterial whether or not any remedy or sanction is provided for the benefit of consumers or not (section 211(4)(b)). For example, in relation to section 211(2)(d), a provision may require that a person must be compensated if another person does, or omits to do, something required by the provision. Also, under the Control of Misleading Advertisements Regulations 1988 a person concerned with the publication of a misleading advertisement may be subject to proceedings for an injunction brought by the DGFT; but there is no express duty on a person not to publish misleading advertisements. It is intended to list the Control of Misleading Advertisements Regulations 1998 in both the Community infringements regime and the domestic infringements regime for the reasons explained below.

494.   Section 211(2)(e) enables the order to specify as within the definition of a domestic infringement things done or omitted to be done where an enactment creates a sanction of unenforceability. An example is the Consumer Credit Act 1974. A large number of 'requirements' of the Consumer Credit Act 1974 have as their sanction the unenforceability (against the debtor or hirer) of the consumer credit agreement or of the security of the agreement, or of rights under them. An example is requirements in relation to the form, content and signature of agreements in sections 60 and 61, and the duty to supply copies of the agreement and notice of the right to cancel in sections 62 to 64. In these cases, the court can allow the agreement to be enforced except in cases set out in sections 127(3) and (4) (e.g. unsigned agreements or where notice of the right to cancel is not given as required).

495.   To the extent that requirements in the Consumer Credit Act 1974 transpose the Consumer Credit Directive (87/102/EEC), they would be covered by the definition of Community infringements in section 212. But the scope of the Consumer Credit Act

1974 goes beyond the giving of effect to the Consumer Credit Directive and 'additional permitted protections' within the meaning of section 212, although it is difficult to draw a clear dividing line. For this reason, it is intended to list the Consumer Credit Act 1974 in both the Community infringements regime and the domestic infringements regime.

496.   Section 211(2)(f) enables an order to specify as within the definition of a domestic infringement any act or omission by which a person supplying goods or services purports or attempts to exercise any right relating to the supply when legislation restricts or excludes him from doing so in such circumstances. *Subsection (2)(f)* covers, for example, the creditor who seeks to enforce a term of a regulated credit agreement when he has failed to comply with a statutory pre-condition for enforcement, such as the requirement to give the debtor or hirer seven days' notice of his intention to do so under section 76 of the Consumer Credit Act 1974. It would also cover cases where a creditor recovers possession of protected hire-purchase goods without a court order, as required by section 90 of the Consumer Credit Act 1974 and the business which claims money or the return of goods under a contract which is unenforceable.

497.   A person who demands or accepts payments of sums when legislation relieves the payee of liability for them would also be purporting to exercise a right within subsection (2)(f). An example is section 93 of the Consumer Credit Act 1974, which provides that a debtor under a consumer credit agreement is not liable to pay increased interest when he is in default.

498.   Section 211(2)(g) enables an order to specify as within the definition of a domestic infringement an act or omission by which a person supplying or seeking to supply goods or services purports or attempts to avoid liability relating to the supply in circumstances where such avoidance is restricted or prevented under an enactment. An example of an enactment which prevents the exclusion of liability is section 2(1) of the Unfair Contract Terms Act 1977. This section provides that contract terms or notices purporting to exclude or restrict liability for death or personal injury resulting from negligence are void and of no effect under all circumstances.

499.   Section 211(3) makes clear that, when specifying acts or omissions within the legislation or common law provisions covered in an order under section 211(2), the Secretary of State may exclude a subcategory of the act or omission concerned from the scope of the order.

500.   The Department intends to make orders defining UK law for the purpose of the definition of a Community infringement, and listing the UK legislation and civil law obligations to which the definition of a domestic infringement will apply, before this Part of the Act comes into force. As with the Injunctions Directive and the way the Office of Fair Trading has used its existing powers under Part III of FTA 1973, the intention is that the list for domestic infringements should initially be limited to breaches of legislation whose main focus is to protect the economic interests of

consumers, together with breaches of contract for the supply of goods or services and of the duty of care in negligence.

501.   As a general rule it would not be the Department's intention to include UK law implementing the directives listed in the annex to the Injunctions Directive in the domestic infringements regime. This is because breach of these will in any case be a Community infringement. However, there will be some cases where this will be necessary, for example, where the Department wants to be sure of covering more than what could be said to transpose listed directives in reliance on the minimum clause. For example, as mentioned above, it is not possible to draw a clear distinction between some of the provisions of the Consumer Credit Act 1974 that implement the consumer credit directive and others that are outside the scope of the directive. It is therefore the Department's intention to list the Consumer Credit Act 1974 in both the Community infringements regime and the domestic infringements regime.

502.   A useful weapon against homeworking or outworking scams has been the Control of Misleading Advertising Regulations 1988, which implement the Misleading Advertising Directive (84/450/EEC). Although prospective business people are protected by this directive, they may not necessarily be 'consumers' for the purpose of the definition of a Community infringement. The Department therefore also intends to include the Control of Misleading Advertisements Regulations 1988 under the domestic infringements regime as well as the Community infringements regime.

Section 213: Enforcers

503.   This section deals with those bodies who are to have enforcement powers under this Part.

504.   Three categories of enforcement bodies are defined: 'general enforcers', 'designated enforcers' and 'Community enforcers'.

505.   'General enforcers' are the OFT, every weights and measures authority in Great Britain (trading standards departments) and the Department of Enterprise, Trade and Investment in Northern Ireland (*subsection (1)*).

506.   The Secretary of State is given an order-making power to confer enforcement powers upon other UK public bodies and private consumers organisations that have as one of their purposes the protection of the collective interests of consumers (*subsection (2)*). These enforcers are termed 'designated enforcers'. An order under this section may designate a body for the purposes of domestic and/or Community infringements, and for different types of infringement within each of those categories (*subsections (6) and (7)*).

507.   The Secretary of State may only confer enforcement powers on a public body if it is independent (*subsection (3)*) and on a private consumer organisation if it fulfils such criteria as the Secretary of State specifies by order (*subsection (4)*). The designation of a body by virtue of subsection (3) will be conclusive evidence that the body is a

public body for the purposes of this Part. This will be relevant, for example, in relation to whether the enforcer is to have the statutory power to obtain documents and information under section 225 (*subsection (8)*).

508.   Regulation 4 of the SNORs contains the existing power to designate private consumer organisations (in the SNORs called 'other UK qualified entities') and sets out criteria according to which they may be designated. It is anticipated the Secretary of State will set similar criteria for designating private consumer organisations for the purposes of this Part. It is open to her to decide to set different criteria in respect of Community and domestic infringements, but at present we do not anticipate this will be the case. The power to designate includes power to revoke the designation from any body which ceases to meet the criteria.

509.   It is intended that the first order made under this section will be to designate the public enforcement authorities (in the SNORs called 'public UK qualified entities'), other than those who are general enforcers under this Part, at present listed in Schedule 3 to the SNORs for Community infringements. These are the statutory regulators for the gas, electricity, water, telecommunications and rail industries, the Information Commissioner and the Civil Aviation Authority. It may also designate any private consumer organisations which have been designated under the SNORs as 'other UK qualified entities' for Community infringements by the time this Part of the Act comes into force.

510.   Community enforcers are entities from other EEA States that are listed in the Official Journal of the European Communities under Article 4.3 of the Injunctions Directive (*subsection (5)*). It is a requirement of the Injunctions Directive that the courts or administrative authorities of an EEA State must accept inclusion in this list as proof of the legal capacity of the entities to apply for injunctions in all EEA States to stop Community infringements.

511.   In the same way, UK enforcers which are designated for the purposes of Community infringements can apply for injunctions in other Member States to protect UK consumers. At the request of a designated enforcer who has been designated for the purposes of one or more Community infringements, the Secretary of State must notify the European Commission that it should be added to the list of bodies published in the Official Journal of the European Communities as being qualified to bring proceedings in all Member States.

512.   The Department considers that the Injunctions Directive only gives enforcement bodies the power to apply for injunctions in other EEA States in respect of those Community infringements for which it is designated in its home State. The notification to the Commission must include the types of Community infringement in respect of which the body is designated, in addition to the name and a general description of the purpose of the body, which are required under Article 4(2) of the Injunctions Directive (*subsection (10)*). It is up to the Commission how it deals with the publication, but the current Official Journal entry (OJ No. C30, 2002, Item 2) for

Denmark includes a reference to the individual directives for which each of the Consumer Ombudsman and Danish Medicines Control Agency are qualified to bring actions.

513.   The Secretary of State is required to notify the Commission if a designated enforcer ceases to be designated for the purpose of Community infringements or if its designation in relation to such infringements is varied. The Secretary of State must also inform the Commission of any change in the name or purpose of a designated enforcer (*subsection (11)*).

Enforcement procedure

Section 214: Consultation

514.   This section applies if an enforcer thinks that an infringement has occurred, is occurring, or, in the case of a Community infringement, is likely to occur. Except where the OFT thinks that an application for an enforcement order should be made without delay, enforcers must first consult the OFT (if it is not the enforcer) and the person against whom the enforcement order may be made and give the latter the opportunity to stop the infringement occurring, continuing or being repeated, as the case may be, without the need for court action (*subsections (1) to (3)*). It may be, for example, that the trader was not aware that his conduct constituted an infringement or that he is able to show that it was an isolated occurrence. The enforcer may then decide it is not necessary to make an application. It may also be that the trader decides to offer an undertaking to the enforcer under section 219.

515.   After the end of 14 days beginning on the day after the request for consultation is received, the enforcer may make an application for an enforcement order under section 215 (subsection (4)(a)). This period is reduced to 7 days where the enforcer intends to make an application for an interim enforcement order (subsection (4)(b)) (see below). The Secretary of State may by order make rules as to consultation (*subsection (5)*). The Department plans to use this to provide for addresses for service of the request for consultation and to specify a deemed date of receipt of a request for consultation, for example two days after posting first class.

516.   The purpose of enforcers being required to consult the OFT is to enable the OFT to perform a co-ordinating role in relation to proceedings under this Part. This will enable the OFT to facilitate the sharing of information between enforcers to promote consistent enforcement throughout the country and to make directions under section 216 to avoid the risk of traders facing multiple actions in relation to the same infringement. It is not envisaged that the OFT should become directly involved in the consultations with the trader except where it is the enforcer or has been asked to do so by the trader.

Section 215: Applications

517.   This section is concerned with the person against whom an application for an enforcement order may be made, the types of infringement in respect of which

particular enforcers are to have the power to make applications to the courts, and the courts that are to hear such proceedings.

518.   An application for an enforcement order (including an interim enforcement order) must name the person the enforcer thinks has engaged or is engaging in conduct that constitutes an infringement, or who is likely to engage in conduct that would constitute a Community infringement (*subsection (1)*).

519.   A general enforcer (that is, the OFT, a trading standards department or the Department of Enterprise, Trade and Investment in Northern Ireland) may make an application for an enforcement order in respect of all infringements to which this Part applies (*subsection (2)*).

520.   A designated enforcer may make an application for an enforcement order only in respect of those infringements for which it is designated (*subsection (3)*).

521.   A Community enforcer may make an application for an enforcement order only in respect of a Community infringement (*subsection (4)*).

522.   An application for an enforcement order may be made to the High Court or a county court if the person against whom the order is sought carries on business or has a place of business in England and Wales or Northern Ireland; or to the Court of Session or the sheriff if the person carries on business or has a place of business in Scotland (*subsection (5)*).

523.   The court may examine whether the purpose of a Community enforcer justifies it taking action in the particular case (*subsection (6)*). Where the court thinks that the purpose of the Community enforcer does not justify it taking action, it may refuse the application solely on that ground (*subsection (7)*). The purpose of a Community enforcer in this context is the purpose of the body for the purpose of the Injunctions Directive. The Department believes that the Injunctions Directive only gives Community enforcers the right to make applications for enforcement orders in respect of those interests protected by the enforcer in its home State. The purpose of a Community enforcer would therefore, in particular, include the infringements in respect of which it has the power to act in its home State (*subsection (8)*).

524.   An enforcer that is not the OFT must notify the OFT of the outcome of an application made under this section (*subsection (9)*). This would include the terms of any undertaking given to, or order made by, the court. This is to assist the OFT in its co-ordination role.

Section 216: Applications: directions by OFT

525.   This section provides that, if the OFT believes that an enforcer or enforcers other than itself intends to apply for an enforcement order in respect of a particular infringement, it may direct which enforcer may bring such proceedings, or that only it may do so (*subsections (1) and (2)*). Where the OFT directs that only it may make such

application, that does not prevent it from seeking a voluntary undertaking from the trader or from taking other steps to bring the infringement to an end (*subsection (3)*). The OFT may vary or withdraw any direction made under this section (*subsection (4)*).

526. The effect is that if the OFT becomes aware that an enforcer (other than a Community enforcer) is intending to make an application, but there are regulatory or self-regulatory mechanisms that the enforcer has not attempted to use, the OFT could make a direction to the effect that only it can make a court application. This will be the case even if the OFT had no prior knowledge, and therefore no intention to apply itself, before it became aware of the alleged infringement or the other enforcer's intention. This will ensure that existing regulatory and self-regulatory mechanisms, such as that operated by the Independent Television Commission (ITC) in relation to broadcast advertising and sponsorship, are not by-passed.

527. The section will also allow the OFT to prevent businesses being faced with multiple applications in respect of the same infringement. The OFT can decide which enforcer is best placed to proceed with the application. It may be, if, for example, a majority of the trader's customers are in another EEA State, that the OFT could direct that if an application is to be made, then it should be a Community enforcer that brings proceedings and not others, but this is not likely to happen very often.

528. The OFT may take such steps as it thinks appropriate for bringing a direction given under this section to the attention of other enforcers who may be affected by it. This will minimise the risk that others will seek to enter into informal negotiations with the trader over the same infringement (*subsection (5)*).

529. This section does not prevent an application for an enforcement order being made by a Community enforcer (*subsection (6)*). This is because the only constraint permitted by the Injunctions Directive on such bodies is the requirement to give the OFT two weeks' notice of their intention to make an application to the courts (see section 214).

Section 217: Enforcement orders

530. Where the court is satisfied that the person against whom proceedings have been brought has engaged in conduct that constitutes an infringement or, in the case of a Community infringement, is likely to do so, the court may make an enforcement order against that person (*subsections (1) to (3)*). The Department considers that it is a requirement of the Injunctions Directive for the courts to be able to make orders to stop threatened Community infringements. This could be the case if an enforcer becomes aware that a misleading advertisement is about to be published in a newspaper or periodical.

531. In considering whether to make an enforcement order, the court must have regard to whether the defendant has failed to comply with any voluntary undertaking given under section 219 relating to any conduct that constitutes an infringement (*subsection (4)*). Failure to comply with an undertaking would be pertinent to the question of

whether an enforcement order should be made (rather than another undertaking accepted). The order must indicate the nature of the conduct that the person has engaged in, or in the case of a Community infringement which is likely to engage in, that constitutes an infringement and must require the person against whom it is made:

- not to continue or repeat the conduct; or

- not to engage in conduct of the nature indicated by the court if it has found that a Community infringement is likely to be committed; and

- not to engage in conduct of the nature indicated by the court in the course of the business concerned or another business carried out by him in future; and

- not to consent to, or connive in, the carrying out of such conduct by a body corporate with which he has a special relationship as defined in section 222(3),

as provided by *subsections (5)-(7)*. The last element means that the defendant must not consent to, or connive in, the carrying out of such conduct by a body corporate of which he is a director or which he controls. This will prevent a sole trader from evading the scope of an enforcement order by acquiring a company with a nominal share capital to operate his business and continue the infringement.

532.   In addition, the court may order the defendant (but not the enforcer) at his expense to publish its order (in full or in part) and/or a corrective statement in such form and manner as deemed adequate with a view to eliminating or reducing the continuing effects of the infringement (*subsection (8)*). The availability of this remedy is a requirement of the Injunctions Directive. An obvious example for its use would be in respect of an advertisement that has been found to be misleading. It would be in the discretion of the courts when to exercise this power and how the information should best be published to bring it to the attention of consumers. However, whether or not the court exercises this power, enforcers would be free to publish the terms of court orders and undertakings given to the court (see below).

533.   As an alternative to making an enforcement order, the court may accept an undertaking from the defendant. The undertaking may take the same form as the order, or may be to take such steps as the court considers will prevent him doing anything the order would have prohibited him from doing (*subsection (9)*). In these circumstances, the court may also accept a further undertaking from the defendant to publish at his expense the terms of the undertaking (in full or in part) or a corrective statement (*subsection (10)*).

534.   Where the court accepts an undertaking from the defendant in respect of conduct that constitutes an infringement, it cannot make an enforcement order in respect of that finding (*subsection (11)*) except where further proceedings are brought under section 220.

535.   An injunction (or interdict in Scotland) generally has effect only in the jurisdiction (England and Wales, or Scotland or Northern Ireland) in which it was granted. The effect of *subsection (12)* is that an enforcement order made under this Part will apply throughout the UK. It will therefore be capable of stopping a person who is the subject of an order in one jurisdiction of the UK from harming the collective interests of consumers in the other two jurisdictions.

536.   This Part makes no special provisions for appeals. The normal rules will apply.

Section 218: Interim enforcement order

537.   This section provides that, where certain conditions are satisfied, the courts may make an interim enforcement order pending the determination of an application for an enforcement order.

538.   Where it is alleged that a person is engaged in conduct that constitutes an infringement, or is likely to engage in conduct that constitutes a Community infringement, and it appears to the court that:

* an application for an enforcement order in respect of the alleged conduct would be likely to be successful; and

* it is expedient that the conduct is prohibited or prevented immediately,

the court may make an interim enforcement order. An interim order may be made without notice being given to the person named in the application if it appears to the court that it is appropriate to do so (*subsection (1)*). But *subsection (7)* requires that where an application for an interim enforcement order is made without notice being given to the person named in the application it must explain why no notice has been given.

539.   An application for an interim enforcement order without notice may be necessary, for example, if an enforcer becomes aware that a misleading advertisement is about to be published in a national newspaper or if a trader sets up in temporary premises to sell goods of unsatisfactory quality or to mislead consumers as to the goods they are purchasing (so-called 'one day sales').

540.   An interim enforcement order must indicate the nature of the alleged conduct and must require the person against whom it is made:

* not to continue or repeat the conduct; or

* not to engage in conduct of the nature indicated by the court if it has found that a Community infringement is likely to be committed; and

* not to engage in conduct of the nature indicated by the court in the course of

the business concerned or another business carried out by him in future; and

- not to consent to, or connive in, the carrying out of such conduct by a body corporate with which he has a special relationship as defined in section 222(3),

as provided by *subsections (2) to (4)*.

541. An interim enforcement order may be applied for before an application for an enforcement order is made and at any time until an application for an enforcement order is determined (*subsection (5)*). However, an enforcer other than the OFT must not make an application for an interim enforcement order without complying with the prior consultation requirements in section 214. A consultation period of 7 days is required under that section unless the OFT agrees that an application should be made without delay. The Department would expect enforcers to obtain OFT's agreement to an application being made without delay in cases of great urgency and whenever an application is made without notice.

542. An application for an interim enforcement order must refer to all matters which are known to the applicant and which are material to the question of whether or not the application should be granted (*subsection (6)*). This will enable the courts to consider all the relevant information known to the applicant when an application for an interim enforcement order is made without notice being given to the person named in the application, or where an application with notice is not defended.

543. The court may vary or discharge an interim enforcement order on the application of either the enforcer who applied for the order or the person against whom it is made (*subsection (8)*). An interim enforcement order ceases to have effect on the determination of the application for an enforcement order (*subsection (9)*).

544. As an alternative to making an interim enforcement order, the court may accept an undertaking from the defendant. The undertaking may take the same form as the interim order, or may be to take such steps as the court considers will prevent him doing anything the order would have prohibited him from doing (*subsection (10)*).

545. As with enforcement orders, an interim enforcement order made in one part of the UK will apply throughout the UK (*subsection (11)*).

Section 219: Undertakings

546. This section provides that where an enforcer has the power to make an application to the court for an enforcement order, it (the enforcer) may accept an undertaking from a person who it believes has engaged, or is engaging, in conduct that constitutes an infringement or, in the case of a Community infringement, is likely to do so (*subsections (1) to (3)*). The undertaking must require that person:

- not to continue or repeat the conduct in question; or

- not to engage in such conduct which is believed to constitute a Community infringement if it has not yet occurred; and

- not to engage in conduct of that kind in the course of the business concerned or another business carried out by him in future; and

- not to consent to, or connive in, the carrying out of conduct of that kind by a body corporate with which he has a special relationship as defined in section 222(3).

as provided by *subsections (4)* and *(5)*. An enforcer may decide that such an undertaking will avoid the need for it to apply for an enforcement order. An enforcer must notify the OFT of the terms of any undertaking given to it under this section and the identity of the person giving it (*subsection (6)*). This is to enable the OFT to fulfil its co-ordination role.

547. If a person gives an undertaking to an enforcer under this section, the court must take this, as well as whether he has failed to comply with it, into account in considering whether to make an enforcement order on any subsequent application.

Section 220: Further proceedings

548. This section applies where an enforcer believes that an enforcement order (including an interim enforcement order) or an undertaking given to the court has been breached. In any such case, either the enforcer who made the application for the order or the OFT will be able to make a further application to the court to enforce the order (*subsections (1) and (2)*).

549. This further application might lead the court to find that its order or undertakings given to it have been breached and therefore that the defendant is in contempt of court. If the court finds that a breach has been committed, it can impose a fine and/or, if the defendant is an individual, a term of imprisonment not exceeding two years.

550. However, where a further application is made to the court in respect of a failure to comply with an undertaking given to the court, the enforcer may instead make an application for an enforcement order or for an interim enforcement order (*subsection (3)*). Similarly, the court may make an enforcement order or an interim enforcement order instead of finding that the defendant is in contempt (*subsection (4)*). An application to enforce an undertaking given to the court must be made to the court that accepted the undertaking (*subsection (5)(b)*).

551. An enforcer (other than the OFT) must notify the OFT if it makes an application to the court in respect of a failure to comply with an enforcement order, an interim enforcement order, or an undertaking given to the court. It must also notify the OFT of any order made by the court on the application (*subsection (6)*). Where an enforcer makes an application for an enforcement order or an interim enforcement order in further proceedings the consultation requirements in section 214 and the OFT's

powers of direction in section 216 do not apply: the purpose of notifying the OFT is to keep it informed of proceedings against particular traders to assist its co-ordination function.

Section 221: Community infringements: proceedings

552. This section has two purposes. First, it provides general enforcers and designated enforcers that are public bodies with any necessary additional powers to their existing statutory powers to enable them to bring proceedings under the legislation implementing the Injunctions Directive in any EEA State to stop Community infringements that originate there but that harm the collective interests of consumers in the UK (*subsections (1) and (2)*). Whether private designated enforcers will have these powers will depend upon their own constitutions.

553. Second, it enables general enforcers and designated enforcers (both public and private) to co-operate with any Community enforcer for the purpose of bringing proceedings in other EEA States and to cooperate with such an enforcer in the exercise of its functions (including accepting undertakings under section 219) under the provisions of this Part (*subsections (3) and (4)*). There is no need for the section to refer explicitly to an enforcer being able to apply jointly with or on behalf of another enforcer because there is no restriction on the enforcer's ability to apply in these circumstances. Whether a body is entitled to bring proceedings and in respect of which infringements is determined by section 213 and any designation order made under it.

Section 222: Bodies corporate: accessories

554. This section provides that if a body corporate engages in conduct that constitutes a domestic or Community infringement with the consent or connivance of a person (an accessory) who has a special relationship with that body corporate, the consent or connivance is also conduct that constitutes the infringement (*subsections (1) and (2)*). The effect is that an application can be made under section 215 for an enforcement order against an accessory who consents to, or connives at, the conduct of the body corporate.

555. The court will have the power to make an order against, or to accept an undertaking from, an accessory whether or not it has made an order or accepted an undertaking from the body corporate (*subsections (5) and (6)*). Similarly, an enforcer may accept an undertaking from an accessory regardless of whether it accepts an undertaking from the body corporate (*subsection (7)*).

556. The provisions of this Part apply to infringements consisting of consent or connivance as they apply to other infringements with the exception that the terms of orders and undertakings are modified slightly by *subsections (8) and (9)* of this section.

557. Where an order is made as referred to in *subsection (5)* or an undertaking is accepted as referred to in *subsections (6) or (7)*, it must require the accessory:

- not to continue to consent to, or connive at, the body corporate's conduct or repeat the consent or connivance;

- not to engage in conduct of the kind committed by the body corporate in the course of any business that may be carried out by him (i.e. as sole trader or in partnership); and

- not to consent to, or connive at, conduct of that kind by any other body corporate with which he has a special relationship, as defined in section 222(3).

558. An accessory may be either a controller of a company or a director, manager, secretary or other similar officer (or a person purporting to act in such a capacity). A 'controller' means someone who instructs the directors of a company as to how to act or someone who, together with any associates, controls one third or more of the voting power in the company *(subsections (3) and (4))*. 'Associate' is defined in subsections (10) to (13) and principally covers husbands and wives, and cohabitees (including ones of the same sex who live together in a settled relationship), relatives and business partners, and companies who share a 'controller'.

Section 223: Bodies corporate: orders

559. Where an enforcement order (including an interim enforcement order) is made against a company, conduct by a company owned by that company or by a sister company would not be a breach of the order. This section will give the court wide power to deal with this situation.

560. This section will empower the court, when making an enforcement order or interim enforcement order under sections 217 or 218, respectively, to direct that the order will be binding upon all other members of a group of interconnected bodies corporate of which it is a member *(subsection (2))*. 'Interconnected bodies corporate' and 'group of interconnected bodies corporate' are defined by reference to the definition of 'subsidiary' in section 736 of the Companies Act 1985 *(subsections (3) to (5))*.

561. Further, if a body corporate subject to an enforcement order (including an interim enforcement order) becomes a member of a group of interconnected bodies corporate subsequently, or the group is enlarged, the enforcer will be able to apply to the court for a direction that the order be binding on the new members or member.

Information

Sections 224 and 225: OFT & Other enforcers

562. These sections provide the OFT, other general enforcers and designated enforcers who are public bodies, with a statutory power to require information (including documents) by means of a notice served on any person.

563. These enforcers will be able to request this information for the purpose of enabling

them to consider whether to exercise their functions under this Part (section 224(2)(a) and section 225(3)(a)). This may be the case, for example, where it is not possible on the basis of *ad hoc* complaints from consumers to determine whether the cause of complaint is the result of an accidental mistake or part of a deliberate pattern of unlawful conduct (e.g. mail order companies sending out goods different from those that were ordered).

564.   These enforcers will also be able to request information for the purpose of monitoring compliance with enforcement orders (including interim enforcement orders) and undertakings, to enable them to decide whether to bring further proceedings under section 220 to enforce a court order or an undertaking given to the court or, in the case of undertakings given to an enforcer, to make an application for an enforcement order (including an interim enforcement order) under section 215. A general enforcer other than the OFT or a designated enforcer that is a public body can only use this power to enable it to exercise any functions it has under this Part (such an enforcer may be designated only in respect of certain kinds of infringement) or to monitor compliance with an enforcement order or undertaking made in proceedings it has brought or with an undertaking given voluntarily to it. No such restriction applies in relation to the OFT, in part because the OFT will have the power to bring a further application to enforce a court order or undertaking given to the court in proceedings brought by any enforcer (section 224(2)(d) and section 225(3)(b)).

565.   Neither designated enforcers that are private bodies nor Community enforcers will have a statutory power to request information themselves. The OFT will therefore have power to request information on behalf of these enforcers to enable them to consider whether to exercise their functions under this Part (section 224(b) and (c)).

Sections 226 and 227: Notices: procedure and enforcement

566.   Section 226 sets out the procedure for notices under sections 224 and 225. They are required to be in writing. In accordance with the ordinary meaning of "writing", notices may in principle be given in electronic communications.

567.   Section 227 sets out the remedies that are available where a notice is not complied with.

568.   If a person fails to furnish the information requested within the time specified, an application may be made by the enforcer that served the notice to the court for an order requiring the default in compliance to be made good. The court for this purpose is a court which may make an enforcement order, that is, the High Court or a county court or their Scottish equivalents.

569.   Where the court is satisfied that the person has failed to comply with a notice and that the information is reasonably required for the purposes set out in sections 224 and 225, it may make an order requiring the person to do anything it is necessary to do to comply with the notice. Where the court makes such an order, it may order costs against the person in default or, if the person is a corporate body, against any of its

officers responsible for the default.

Miscellaneous

Section 228: Evidence

570. *Subsection (1)* provides that convictions in any related criminal proceedings in the UK may be used as evidence in proceedings under this Part.

571. *Subsection (2)* enables findings in civil proceedings to be admitted in evidence under this Part of acts or omissions which constitute Community infringements or certain kinds of domestic infringements, except where the findings have been overturned on appeal (*subsection (3)*).

572. This will allow judgements in the criminal courts and findings in the civil courts to be admitted in evidence for the purpose of proving a breach of the relevant legislation or common law obligations. But it will still be necessary to prove that the conduct harms the collective interests of consumers.

Section 229: Advice and information

573. The OFT is required (as soon as is reasonably practicable) to prepare and publish advice and information explaining the provisions of this Part and indicating how it expects them to operate in practice. The advice and information may include advice and information about the factors the OFT may take into account in considering how to exercise its functions under this Part, such as adherence to the principles of best practice in enforcement as set out in the Enforcement Concordat or any document which replaces it. This will promote consistent enforcement across the country. In preparing any advice and information, the OFT must consult such persons as it considers representative of those affected. This advice and information may be published in such form and in such manner as the OFT considers appropriate. The OFT may at any time publish revised or new advice and information to reflect experience gained in the operation of this Part.

Section 230: Notice to OFT of intended prosecution

574. This section will apply if a local weights and measures authority (ie trading standards department) in England and Wales intends to start proceedings for an offence under an enactment or subordinate legislation which the Secretary of State has specified for the purposes of this section (*subsection (1)*).

575. The authority must give the OFT notice of its intention to start proceedings, together with a summary of the facts on which the charges are to be founded (*subsection (2)*). The authority must not start proceedings until the earlier of the end of 14 days from giving the notice or the day the OFT notifies the authority that it has received the notice and the summary of the facts (*subsection (3)*). The authority must also notify the OFT of the outcome of the proceedings (*subsection (4)*).

576. This section reflects the existing requirements about notices of intended prosecution

in section 130 of the FTA 1973 which relates to offences under the Trade Descriptions Act 1968, Part III of the Consumer Protection Act 1987, the Property Misdescriptions Act 1991 and the Timeshare Act 1992. The Department's intention is to list in the order under section 230 all the legislation providing for criminal offences which will be included in the legislation specified in orders made under sections 211 and 212 in relation to domestic and Community infringements. The purpose is to reinforce the OFT's co-ordination role in respect of the legislation to which this Part applies. For example, the OFT could inform one authority that another is prosecuting or that an enforcement order has been granted. This may lead the authority to decide it is not necessary to prosecute. Proceedings will not however be invalid simply by virtue of the fact that the prosecuting authority has not given the OFT the required notice of intended prosecution.

577.   This section does not apply in relation to Scotland, where all criminal prosecutions are brought by the Procurator Fiscal, or to Northern Ireland where public law enforcement of consumer protection legislation rests with the Department of Enterprise, Trade and Investment.

Section 231: Notice of convictions and judgments to OFT

578.   This section will give the courts in the UK the power to notify the OFT of convictions and judgments that might not otherwise be brought to its attention, for the purpose of the OFT considering whether to exercise its functions under this Part or under the Estate Agents Act 1979 ('EAA'). It is immaterial that proceedings have been finally been disposed of by the courts. Under the EAA, the DGFT has the power to issue a warning notice or a banning order preventing a person from acting as an estate agent. This section will replace section 131 of the FTA 1973.

Interpretation

Section 232: Goods and services

579.   *Subsections (2) and (3)* provide a definition of 'goods' and the 'supply of services' for purposes of this Part, including in relation to the meaning of a 'consumer' in relation to a domestic infringement. These definitions are identical in substance to those contained in section 137(2) of the FTA 1973.

580.   *Subsections (4) and (5)* make provision as to the circumstances in which the supply of goods or services wholly or partly outside the UK are to be regarded as being supplied to a consumer in the UK, so that the provisions on domestic infringements will apply to those transactions. This is when goods or services are supplied in accordance with the arrangements falling within subsection (5), but those arrangements may be made by any means, including electronic means, for example, internet transactions and transactions made by other forms of electronic communications. There is no presumption that a consumer should normally be resident in the UK. The effect is that an application can be made for an enforcement order under section 215 against an e-trader based in the UK whose unlawful conduct which constitutes a domestic infringement is directed at consumers anywhere in the world. *Subsections (4) and (5)*

update an equivalent provision in section 138(3) of the FTA 1973 which does not reflect today's world of e-commerce.

Section 233: Person Supplying Goods

581. This section repeats in substance section 138(4) and 138(5) of the FTA 1973. It provides that in relation to the supply of goods under a hire-purchase agreement, credit sale agreement or conditional sale agreement, the person conducting the antecedent negotiations, as well as the owner or seller, shall be treated as a person supplying or seeking to supply the goods. The effect is that in these types of agreements the dealer will be treated as the supplier as well as the finance company which is technically the supplier under the contract with the consumer.

Section 234: Supply of services

582. This section follows the definition of 'supply of services' in section 137(3) of the FTA 1973, with two modifications. The first modification is the inclusion of new *subsection (4)*, which provides that the supply of services includes making arrangements for a person to receive computer software or data such as information, music or photographs. This is intended to cover electronic supply. Such persons are not receiving anything in physical form and so might not otherwise be receiving 'goods'. This provision ensures that such consumers will be considered to be receiving a service.

583. The second change is the omission from the definition of 'supply of services' of provisions corresponding to sections 137(3)(c), (d), (e) and (g) of FTA 1973, which relate to the making of arrangements to permit the use of land in certain specified circumstances. The Secretary of State is however given a power by order to extend the definition of the supply of services involving arrangements permitting the use of land as in section 137(3A) of the FTA 1973. It is intended that this order-making power will be used to reinstate those provisions relating to the use of land in section 137(3) that are relevant to this Part before this Part of the Act comes into force.

Crown

Section 236: Crown

584. The directives listed in the annex to the Injunctions Directive are binding on the Crown in so far as it carries on activities that bring it within the class of persons who can commit Community infringements. No distinction is made between domestic and Community infringements: the whole Part binds the Crown.

PART 9: INFORMATION

Introduction

585. This Part creates a new gateway and sets out general restrictions and conditions for the disclosure of specified information held by public authorities. It reflects the

Government strategy of widening and harmonising the gateways through which information can be disclosed in the UK and overseas and at the same time introduces appropriate safeguards in respect of permitted disclosure of information.

586. The Anti-Terrorism, Crime and Security Act 2001 introduced a new gateway (and amended numerous existing gateways) to allow the disclosure of certain information within the UK and to overseas authorities for the purpose of pursuing criminal investigations or proceedings. The provisions in this Part create a corresponding gateway for disclosure of information relating to consumer and competition matters for the purpose of criminal investigations and proceedings in the UK and overseas. However, they also create a gateway to allow certain information to be disclosed for facilitating the exercise of certain statutory functions in the UK, and for certain civil investigations and proceedings overseas. This wider gateway is necessary for the disclosure of information relating to consumer and competition matters as overseas enforcement of such legislation is often under a civil regime. The provisions relating to the consumer legislation specified in the Anti-Terrorism, Crime and Security Act 2001 will be repealed when Part 9 of this Act comes into force, and consumer legislation will then be covered by this Part.

587. Within the UK, the provisions in this Part will enable a public authority to disclose information to facilitate the exercise of its own statutory functions and certain statutory functions of other persons and for the purposes of any criminal investigations or proceedings.

588. With regards to overseas public authorities, the provisions are more limited. It will be possible to disclose information to any overseas authority for the purpose of any criminal investigations or proceedings. However, for the purpose of civil proceedings, information can only be disclosed to those public bodies involved in the enforcement of consumer or competition legislation. In addition, competition information obtained under the Financial Services and Markets Act 2000 and certain sensitive commercial information (for example, information connected to market and merger investigations) is expressly excluded from the overseas gateway. There are also various safeguards in this Part designed to prevent the misuse of any information disclosed overseas.

589. In order to provide a consistent regime, the gateways that exist in current legislation for the disclosure of information relating to consumer and competition matters will be harmonised. Therefore, the provisions in this Part will replace the existing information disclosure provisions in the legislation listed in section 247.

Restrictions on disclosure

Section 237: General restriction

590. This section sets out the general restriction on the disclosure of information by a public authority. The term 'public authority' is defined in section 238 by reference to

the Human Rights Act 1998.

591. *Subsection (1)* states that the general restriction applies only to information classed as 'specified information'– as defined in section 238. Therefore, these provisions impose no restrictions on the disclosure of information that falls outside the definitions in section 238. The restriction applies in respect of specified information that relates to either the affairs of an individual or to those of any business of an undertaking.

592. *Subsection (2)* provides that the restriction will apply throughout the lifetime of any individual who is the subject of the information, or while any undertaking to which the information relates continues in existence. However, it also acts as a pointer to the exceptions to the general restriction that are set out in sections 239-243 inclusive.

593. *Subsection (3)* sets out a further exception to the general restriction: disclosure is permitted where the information concerned has already been placed in the public domain by any lawful means, including – but not restricted to – any of the exceptions to the general restriction set out in sections 239-243 inclusive.

594. *Subsection (4)* states that all of the provisions on disclosure of information are subject to the provisions of the Data Protection Act 1998.

595. *Subsection (5)* states that the Competition Appeal Tribunal is not subject to the disclosure provisions of this Part.

596. *Subsection (6)* confirms that the restrictions on disclosure, with the exception of section 244, are not intended to affect any power or duty to disclose information which exists outside Part 9 of the Act (i.e. whether arising under this Act or elsewhere).

Section 238: Information
597. This section defines the information to which the disclosure provisions will apply.

598. *Subsection (1)* defines 'specified information' as information that has been obtained by a 'public authority' (as defined in subsection (3)) in connection with the exercise by it of any function that it has under the following Parts of this Act - Part 1 ('The Office of Fair Trading'), Part 3 ('Mergers'), Part 4 ('Market Investigations'), Part 6 ('Cartel Offence'), Part 7 ('Miscellaneous Competition Provisions') and Part 8 ('Enforcement of Certain Consumer Legislation'), under any of the enactments listed in Schedule 14 of this Act; or under any secondary legislation specified by the Secretary of State in an order. *Subsection (4)* provides that the term "enactment" will be taken to refer to both primary and secondary legislation, including Scottish and Northern Ireland legislation.

599. *Subsection (2)* has the effect of applying the new disclosure provisions to all "specified information" held by public authorities after the passing of this Act, as well

as to information already held by a public authority at the time the Act was passed.

600. *Subsection (3)* requires the term 'public authority' to be construed in accordance with the terms of section 6 of the Human Rights Act 1998 – that is to include courts and tribunals (including the House of Lords in its judicial capacity), as well as any person exercising functions of a public nature, but excluding Parliament. (An 'overseas public authority' is separately defined in section 243 of this Act).

601. *Subsection (5) and (6)* empower the Secretary of State to amend the lists of legislation in Schedule 14, under which statutory functions arise. This will allow the lists to be updated to reflect subsequent changes to the legislative base. *Subsection (7)* provides that statutory instruments made under subsection (4) will be subject to the negative Parliamentary procedure.

Permitted disclosure

Section 239: Consent

602. *Subsection (1)* provides that disclosure will be permitted where the authority wishing to disclose the information obtains the necessary consent(s) that are detailed in the following subsections.

603. *Subsection (2)* requires the consent to disclosure by the provider of the information, but applies only where the authority knows the identity of the person from whom it obtained the information. This recognises the possibility that it may not always be possible to identify the provider of particular pieces of information. Where the identity of the provider is known, the authority must satisfy itself that the provider was legally in possession of the information and that the provider consents to further disclosure before releasing the information.

604. *Subsections (3), (4) and (5)* require the consent by the subject of the information. Where the information concerns the affairs of an individual, that individual must consent to further disclosure by the authority. Where the information relates to the business of an undertaking, *subsection (5)* requires consent to be given by a senior representative of the undertaking: for example, the company secretary or other director; a partner; or, in the case of an unincorporated body, a person in a position of management or control.

Section 240: Community obligations

605. This section sets out the principle that disclosure may be made where it is necessary for the authority to disclose the information for the purpose of fulfilling any obligation under European Community law.

Section 241: Statutory functions

606. This section enables public authorities holding information to disclose specified information to persons exercising specified statutory functions.

607. *Subsection (1)* provides that a public authority that holds information to which the disclosure provisions in this Part apply may disclose that information for the purpose of facilitating the exercise by that public authority of any of its statutory functions.

608. *Subsection (2)* provides that if information is disclosed under subsection (1) in circumstances in which it is not put into the public domain (for example where it is not published in the press), such information must not be further disclosed by the recipient of the information without the agreement of the public authority that disclosed the information to it, and disclosure may only be for the purpose of facilitating the exercise by the public authority that made the original disclosure of its statutory functions.

609. *Subsection (3)* provides that specified information held by public authorities can be disclosed to any person for the purpose of facilitating the exercise of any function that that person has under this Act, any of the Acts specified in Schedule 15 or any secondary legislation specified by the Secretary of State by an order made for the purpose of this subsection.

610. *Subsection (4)* provides that information disclosed to a person exercising a function under one of the Acts or pieces of legislation specified in subsection (3) can only be used for a purpose relating to that function.

611. *Subsection (5)* provides that the term 'enactment' will be taken to refer to both primary and secondary legislation, including Scottish and Northern Ireland legislation.

612. *Subsection (6)* empowers the Secretary of State to amend the lists of enactments in Schedule 15.

613. *Subsection (8)* provides that statutory instruments made under *subsection (6)* will be subject to the negative Parliamentary procedure.

Section 242: Criminal proceedings
614. This section permits disclosure for the purposes of criminal proceedings.

615. *Subsection (1)* permits a public authority to disclose specified information to any person for the purposes of investigating whether there have been breaches of UK criminal law; assisting in the bringing or conducting of UK criminal proceedings; or deciding whether to commence or terminate such investigations or proceedings. Disclosure is not required to be for the purposes of specified statutory functions – information may be disclosed for the purpose of the enforcement of any enactment by way of criminal proceedings.

616. *Subsection (2)* provides that information disclosed under this section can only be used for the purpose for which it is disclosed.

617. *Subsection (3)* provides that a public authority may only make a disclosure under

section 242 if it is satisfied that the disclosure is proportionate to what is sought to be achieved by it.

Section 243: Overseas disclosures

618.   This section specifies the circumstances under which information may be disclosed to overseas authorities.

619.   *Subsections (1), (2) and (12)* permit a public authority to disclose specified information to any overseas public authority (as defined in *subsection (11)*) for the purpose of any criminal investigations or proceedings, or for civil investigations or proceedings that relate to competition or consumer matters. *Subsection (12)* specifically provides that disclosure may be made for the purposes of overseas civil proceedings under legislation that is equivalent to the domestic infringements and Community infringements set out in Part 8 of the Act.

620.   *Subsection (3)* prevents the disclosure to any overseas authority of information that is held by any person or body that has been designated as an enforcer by the Secretary of State for the purposes of Part 8 of this Act under *subsection* 213(4). It also prevents the disclosure to any overseas authority of any competition information obtained under the Financial Services and Markets Act 2000 and certain sensitive commercial information (for example, information connected to market and merger investigations).

621.   *Subsection (4)* provides that the Secretary of State can prevent disclosure of information overseas if she thinks the proceedings or investigation for which the information has been requested would be more appropriately carried out by authorities in the UK or in another country. *Subsection (5)* requires the Secretary of State to take appropriate steps to bring any decision made by him under *subsection (4)* to the attention of persons likely to be affected by it.

622.   *Subsection (6)* sets out the considerations that a public authority must take into account when deciding whether to disclose information overseas, namely whether the reason for the request is sufficiently serious to justify disclosure; the existence of appropriate protection against self-incrimination in criminal proceedings and for personal data in the requesting country; and the existence of any mutual assistance agreements covering the information concerned with the requesting country.

623.   *Subsection (7)* states that protection against self-incrimination and of personal data will be appropriate if it corresponds to that provided in any part of the UK.

624.   *Subsections (8) and (9)* give the Secretary of State the power, by order (subject to the negative resolution procedure) to modify, add to, or remove any of the considerations in *subsection (6)*.

625.   *Subsection (10)* prevents information that is disclosed to overseas authorities from being further disclosed (without the permission of the UK authority from whom the

information came). This prevents the overseas authority from using the information for any purpose other than the purpose for which it is disclosed by the UK public authority and from further disclosing it to other bodies or authorities. Should they wish to use it for a different purpose than that originally specified, a further request to the UK authority would have to be made.

626. It is accepted that *subsection (10)(a)* and *(b)* are essentially unenforceable as there are no sanctions that could be taken against an overseas authority that contravenes these conditions. However, it is envisaged that should an overseas authority breach these provisions it is unlikely that a UK authority would disclose any further information.

627. *Subsection (11)* defines an overseas public authority. For the purpose of this Part, an overseas public authority is any organisation involved in the conduct of criminal investigations or proceedings, and also those organisations involved in the conduct of any civil investigations or proceedings related to the enforcement of competition or consumer legislation. In reality, this will probably include police and security forces together with national competition authorities and organisations with powers linked to consumer legislation (these could be public or private bodies).

Section 244: Specified information: considerations relevant to disclosure

628. This section sets out further considerations to which public authorities must have regard before disclosing any specified information (whether under a power in Part 9 or elsewhere).

629. *Subsections (2) and (3)* provide that, before disclosing the relevant information, a public authority must consider whether disclosure would be contrary to the public interest, and whether disclosure would cause significant harm to the interests of the business or individual to which it relates.

630. *Subsection (4)* provides that, should the public authority consider that disclosure of particular information could significantly harm the interests of an individual or a business, then they must make a judgement as to the extent to which disclosure of that information is necessary.

Offences

Section 245: Offences

631. This section sets out the circumstances in which the disclosure of information, or the use of information disclosed, constitutes an offence, and also specifies the sanctions that will apply if such an offence is committed.

632. *Subsection (1)* explains that an offence is committed if specified information is disclosed in circumstances to which none of the relevant exceptions set out in this Part applies and whilst the individual who is the subject of the information is still alive or any undertaking to which the information relates continues to trade.

633.   *Subsection (2)* specifies that an offence is also committed if information is disclosed overseas despite a direction from the Secretary of State that it should not be.

634.   *Subsection (3)* extends the offence to include the use of information for a purpose not permitted under this Part.

635.   *Subsection (4)* specifies the maximum prison terms and fines for an offence under Part 9.

Schedule 14: Specified functions

636.   This Schedule specifies the Acts under which any information obtained by a public authority in connection with the exercise of any statutory function will be 'specified information' for the purposes of this Part.

Schedule 15: Enactments conferring functions

637.   This Schedule lists certain legislation under which statutory functions arise for the purpose of section 241. Information may only be passed to a public authority for the purpose of carrying out a statutory function that arises under the enactments listed in this Schedule.

PART 10: INSOLVENCY

638.   The provisions in the Act form part of the Government's ongoing strategy for dealing with the consequences of indebtedness and modernising the court's role in dealing with insolvency. In July 2001, the Government published its White Paper, 'Productivity and Enterprise: Insolvency – A Second Chance'. This built on an ongoing trend established by the Cork Report[1] to promote a culture of company rescue, and continued through the introduction of Insolvency Acts of 1986 and 2000. The White paper also built on The Insolvency Service consultation paper, 'Bankruptcy – A Fresh Start', published in April 2000.

639.   The insolvency sections fall into four main sections: corporate insolvency; the abolition of Crown preference; individual insolvency (bankruptcy and individual voluntary arrangements) and the financial arrangements relating to the functions performed by the Secretary of State in relation to insolvency. These notes provide a general commentary on what the legislation seeks to achieve.

Companies etc.

640.   Changes to the existing corporate insolvency regime focus on restricting the use of administrative receivership and streamlining administration. The White Paper *'Productivity and Enterprise: Insolvency – A Second Chance'* recognised that the

---

[1] Insolvency Law & Practice: Report of the Review Committee (Cork Report) (1982) CMND 8558

administration procedure introduced by the Insolvency Act 1986 was seen as an important tool in providing companies in financial difficulties with a breathing space in which to put a rescue plan to creditors. However, it also recognised that the procedure could be improved.

641.   The existing provisions contained in Part II of the Insolvency Act 1986 allow the court to make an administration order in respect of a company that is in financial difficulties. Broadly speaking, the effect of such an order is to afford the company protection from its creditors whilst attempts are made to save the company or achieve a better result for creditors than would be achieved in a winding-up. However, in practice, in many cases where a company gets into financial difficulties, this will lead to the appointment of an administrative receiver by those providing financial support for the company (typically the company's bank), since they usually will have taken a floating charge over all the company's assets. The holder of a floating charge has an effective veto over the appointment of an administrator. Such a person must be given notice of any application for an administration order, and if he or she appoints an administrative receiver, the court must dismiss the application unless the appointor of the administrative receiver consents to the making of an administration order (see section 9(2)(a) and section 9(3) Insolvency Act 1986).

642.   An administrative receiver primarily owes duties to his or her appointor rather than the company's creditors as a whole (as to the duties owed by an administrative receiver see *Medforth v Blake* [1999] 2 BCLC 221). His or her primary function is to seek repayment of the debt owed to his or her appointor. An administrative receiver has no powers or duty to seek to put together a company rescue in the same way that an administrator has (an administrator, both under the old procedure and as amended by this Act, may put proposals to creditors for a Company Voluntary Arrangement (CVA) pursuant to Part I of the Insolvency Act 1986 or a scheme of arrangement pursuant to section 425 Companies Act 1985) (see sections 8(3) and 23 of the Insolvency Act 1986).

643.   The sections will alter the above provisions in the following way. First, the appointment of administrative receivers will be restricted to certain exceptions (existing arrangements and capital markets) and the Act seeks to provide that administrators will in future be appointed in situations that would have been dealt with through administrative receivership. Second, the procedure has been amended to streamline the process both in the provisions of the Act and the Rules made under section 411 Insolvency Act 1986 that seek to give effect to the provisions of the Act. Perhaps the most obvious of the measures is the introduction of the non-court routes into administration. The procedure has been amended to provide a single purpose made up of a hierarchy of three objectives and expressly to provide that the administrator must carry out his or her functions in the interests of all the creditors. It was recognised that the administration procedure as it stood prior to commencement of the relevant parts of this Act was to a degree cumbersome.

644.   Administration will continue to have many of the features of the current system. At

Annex E there is a table of correspondence that will assist readers in identifying to what extent the provisions of the Insolvency Act 1986 are reflected in new Schedule B1.

Section 248 & Schedule 16: Replacement of Part II of Insolvency Act 1986

645. In order to provide for the streamlining of administration, section 248 replaces Part II of the Insolvency Act 1986 with a new Schedule B1 - as set out in Schedule 16 of this Act. This will be inserted after Schedule A1 to the Insolvency Act 1986. The paragraphs referred to below are paragraphs in Schedule B1.

General effect of Section 248 and Schedule 16: Nature of administration

646. In general terms, the effect of section 248 and Schedule 16 is as follows. Whether or not appointed by the court, an administrator is an officer of the court (as well as an agent of the company) and can only be appointed if qualified to act as an insolvency practitioner. An administrator may not be appointed if the company is already in administration. Generally, a company cannot go into administration if:

- a resolution for voluntary winding-up has been passed (see paragraph 8(1)(a)); or

- a winding-up order has been made (subject to an application by the liquidator or a floating charge holder) (see paragraph 8(1)(b)).

The purpose of administration

647. In order to clarify the purpose of administration and to place greater emphasis on company rescue, paragraph 3 replaces the existing four statutory purposes under section 8(3) Insolvency Act 1986. Under a single overarching purpose, which will apply to all cases of administration, the administrator will be required, where he or she thinks it is reasonably practicable, to carry out his or her functions with the objective of rescuing the company as a going concern (rescuing the company in this context is intended to mean the company and as much of its business as possible). Where that is not reasonably practicable or that objective would not provide the best result for the company's creditors as a whole, the administrator may pursue the second objective referred to below. A hypothetical example of a reasonably practicable rescue might be:

> **Company A** is operating at a profit and has excellent products, a loyal customer base and a healthy order book. However, major investment in a new IT system, which is late and over-budget, has knocked the company off its business plan, its cash flow has suffered and it is unable to pay its debts. The company has been placed in administration and the administrator has had an offer for its business that would provide sufficient funds to pay the secured

creditors and give 35p in the pound for unsecured creditors. However, the administrator has determined that the problems are short-term and they can be resolved and will not have any ongoing effect. The company's bankers have given their support to the administrator's plans to continue trading, the company's business is profitable and the administrator is confident that the company can be rescued by trading its way out of its current financial difficulties, and provide 65p in the pound return for unsecured creditors within 12 months. The administrator puts his or her proposal to the creditors.

648. An example of a case where a rescue would not be reasonably practicable is one where it is clear that the only viable options depend on the continuing support of the company's bankers. The administrator knows that this support will not be forthcoming and that there is no alternative means of financing the company. Whether a company rescue is a reasonably practicable option is a matter of commercial judgment and, on the basis of the case law in relation to similar decisions under the administration procedure prior to commencement of the relevant parts of this Act, it is envisaged that the courts will not seek to criticise the exercise of the administrator's commercial judgement, except in cases where bad faith can be established or the decision taken was one that no reasonable administrator would have taken. (As to the courts' attitude in relation to commercial matters, see for example, re: T&D Industries plc (in administration) [2000] 1 BCLC 471.)

649. Company rescue is most likely to involve the creditors agreeing to the company entering a CVA or a scheme of arrangement under section 425 of the Companies Act 1985. For the purpose of these sections, a proposal that would result in a 'shell' company remaining would not be considered a rescue.

650. If the administrator thinks that a company rescue is not reasonably practicable, or would not achieve the best result for the creditors as a whole, he or she will seek a better result for the creditors than on a winding-up. This might encompass situations where the company's individual businesses are broken up and sold to one or more buyers as going concerns in order to achieve this better result for creditors. Assets of the company may also be sold other than on a going concern basis. A hypothetical example might be:

Company B has good products, and a sound customer base. The company is making losses, its plant and machinery are outdated, and its overheads and debts have been rising for some time. The company has been placed in administration and the administrator has determined that there are no funds available to maintain its entire trading operation or invest in new machinery and it is therefore not reasonably practicable to rescue the company. The administrator has reviewed the company and determined that a sale of its businesses on a going concern basis would provide a better return than a break-up sale of its assets. The administrator markets the businesses and the best offer he or she receives would provide sufficient funds to pay the secured creditors and give 40p in the pound for unsecured creditors. The administrator reports to the creditors at a meeting and explains why it was not reasonably practicable to rescue the company.

651.   The purpose specified in paragraph 3(1)(c) deals mainly with those cases where the company is not viable and has no business that can be sold as a going concern. All that can be done is to sell the company's remaining assets in order to make a distribution to one or more secured or preferential creditors. A hypothetical example might be:

> **Company C** is a service company whose business and reputation were built around its excellent standards of customer service. But a number of key personnel have recently left, the quality of the company's service and its reputation have suffered badly, customers have become dissatisfied and the company is no longer able to attract and retain business. It has been making losses for a number of months and is unable to pay its debts. The company is then placed in administration. The administrator reviews the company and concludes that its business is not viable and a sale is not possible. The administrator markets the company's assets and realises funds that are sufficient to make a part-payment to the secured creditors, and there are no funds available to pay unsecured creditors, except for those resulting from the operation of the ring-fence (see section 252). The administrator reports to the creditors and explains why it was not reasonably practicable to achieve either a company rescue or a better return for unsecured creditors.

652.   An administrator must have regard to the interests of all creditors. In situations under paragraph 3(1)(c) where there are insufficient funds to pay the unsecured creditors, the administrator may only act if he or she does not unnecessarily harm their interests.

Appointment of administrator

653.   Currently, administrators can only be appointed by court order (see section 8 Insolvency Act 1986, as originally enacted), and this route into administration has been retained. However, in order to speed up the process, paragraphs 14-34 set out provisions for the holders of floating charges and companies or their directors to appoint administrators without a court hearing. A diagram showing the out-of-court routes into administration is at Annex F.

General Restrictions

654.   Paragraphs 6-9 set out instances where the appointment of an administrator is not allowed. These restrictions are included for practical reasons, e.g. the administrator must be qualified to act as an insolvency practitioner; the company must not already be in administration; and the company must not be in liquidation, although the

latter restriction can be overruled in certain cases. Paragraph 9 refers to certain types of companies in relation to which the administration procedure applies in a somewhat modified form (see section 422 of the Insolvency Act 1986 and section 360 of the Financial Services and Markets Act 2000), hence the unmodified provisions of Schedule B1 do not apply.

Appointment by court

655.   Paragraphs 10-13 set out the court route into administration. A company or its directors, or one or more creditors of a company (which could include a floating charge holder) can apply to court for an administration order (see paragraph 12). The court may only make an order if it is satisfied that the company is, or is likely to become, unable to pay its debts and that the order is reasonably likely to achieve an objective/the purpose of administration (see paragraph 11).

656.   Paragraph 12(2) provides that, once an administration application has been made, the applicant must notify, amongst others, anyone who has appointed, or is entitled to appoint, either an administrative receiver or an administrator. The application for administration cannot be withdrawn without the permission of the court (see paragraph 12(3)).

657.   On hearing an application for administration, the court may either make the order, dismiss the application or make any other order deemed appropriate, including treating the application as a winding-up petition or making an interim order (paragraph 13).

Appointment by the holder of a floating charge

658.   Paragraphs 14-21 set out the out-of-court route into administration for the holders of floating charges. Floating charge holders will be able to appoint an administrator of their choosing, provided that:

- the floating charge on which the appointment relies is enforceable (see paragraph 16). In this context, enforceable means that the floating charge holder is entitled to call in their security;

- he or she has given notice to the holder of any floating charge which has priority over his or her own floating charge (see paragraph 15);

- the company is not in liquidation (see paragraph 8(1)(a) and (b)) nor has a provisional liquidator been appointed (see paragraph 17(a)); and

- neither an administrative receiver (see paragraph 17(b)) nor administrator is already in office (see paragraph 7).

659. Before the administrator takes office, the floating charge holder must file a notice of appointment with the court (see paragraph 18(1)) identifying the administrator and including a statement from the administrator consenting to the appointment (paragraph 18(3)). Attached to this will be a statutory declaration (paragraph 18(2)) by the floating charge holder stating that they have a qualifying floating charge - which may be one or more floating charges (together with other security) - over the whole or substantially the whole of the company's property and that this is or was enforceable on the date of the appointment (as to when the holder of a floating charge can appoint an administrator, see paragraph 14).

Appointment by company or directors

660. Paragraphs 22-34 set out the out-of-court entry route into administration for companies or the directors of companies. A company or its directors will only be able to appoint an administrator if:

- the company has not been in administration (instigated by the company or directors) (see paragraph 23(2)) nor subject to a moratorium in respect of a failed CVA under Schedule A1 to the Insolvency Act 1986 in the previous 12 months (see paragraph 24(3));

- the company is or is likely to become unable to pay its debts (see paragraph 27(2)(a));

- there is no outstanding winding-up petition or application for administration in respect of the company (see paragraph 25(a));

- the company is not in liquidation (see paragraph 8(1)(a) and (b)); and

- there is no administrator or administrative receiver in office (see paragraphs 6 and 25(c)).

661. The 'notice of intention to appoint' will also identify the proposed administrator (paragraph 26(3)). Once the 'notice of intention to appoint' is sent to the floating charge holder and filed at court, an interim moratorium commences (paragraph 44(2)).

662. During the notice period, a floating charge holder entitled to appoint an administrator may either agree to the proposed appointment or appoint their choice of administrator (paragraph 14). The company or directors must give floating charge holders at least five business days' notice in writing of their intention to appoint an administrator in

this way (paragraph 26). The 'notice of intention to appoint' must also be filed with the court and accompanied by a statutory declaration, stating that the application meets the criteria set out in paragraph 27(2).

663. If the floating charge holder consents to the company's or directors' nominee or does not respond to the notice within five business days, the company/directors must make the appointment no more than ten business days after filing their 'notice of intention to appoint' (paragraph 28(2)). If the 'notice of appointment' is not filed within this period, the interim moratorium will cease to have effect and an administrator cannot be appointed. If there is no floating charge holder, the company/directors file the 'notice of appointment' at court together with a statutory declaration stating that the application meets the criteria set out in paragraph 27.

664. In both cases, this must be accompanied by a statement from the administrator consenting to act and stating that, in their opinion, the purpose of administration is reasonably likely to be achieved. Following this, the administrator is automatically appointed and takes office once the 'notice of appointment' and accompanying documents are filed at court. The company or directors must then notify the administrator of their appointment.

665. If, for whatever reason, the administrator's appointment is discovered to be invalid, the court may order the person who made the appointment to indemnify the administrator against liability (paragraph 34).

Administration application – special cases

666. Paragraph 35 provides for a floating charge holder to apply to court for an administration order without the need to demonstrate that a company is or is likely to become unable to pay its debts. However, the court must be satisfied that the applicant would be entitled to appoint under paragraph 14 (out-of-court appointment by the holder of the floating charge).

667. If there is a winding-up order in relation to the company that would prevent an out-of-court appointment, the floating charge holder can still apply for administration through the court. If an administration order is made, the court will then discharge the winding-up order (paragraph 37). The liquidator may present an application for administration (paragraph 38).

668. Paragraph 39 sets out that, if an administrative receiver (AR) is in office, the court must dismiss an application for administration unless:

- the appointee of the AR consents to the administration order; or

- the court thinks that the appointee's security may be set aside if an administration order were made.

Effect of administration

669.   Paragraph 40 provides that, if the court makes an administration order, it shall dismiss any outstanding winding-up petitions that have not already been dealt with. However, if a company goes into administration as a result of a floating charge holder's appointment of an administrator, then any winding-up petition that has not been dealt with shall be suspended.

670.   As already mentioned, paragraph 39 sets out that, if an AR is in office, the court must dismiss an application for administration unless the appointee of the AR consents to the administration order or the court thinks that the appointee's security may be set aside if an administration order were made. Paragraph 41 provides that, on the making of an administration order, an AR will vacate office, and a receiver will do so if requested by the administrator. The paragraph also secures the AR's and receiver's right to remuneration and any entitlement to an indemnity that they may have had, ahead of the claims of the security-holder who appointed them. However, the right to payment is subject to the moratorium under paragraph 43.

671.   Paragraphs 42 and 43 provide that, once a company is in administration (i.e. an administration order has been made or the administrator has been appointed following the relevant filings by the directors, the company or the qualifying floating charge holder), the moratorium, which is a feature of administration, takes effect. Under paragraph 42 this means that a resolution cannot be passed, or an order made, to wind up the company except in certain circumstances (i.e. compulsory winding-up orders made on public interest petitions).

672.   Paragraph 43 provides that no steps to enforce their rights can be taken by creditors without the consent of the administrator or the permission of the court.

673.   Paragraph 44 provides that the moratorium referred to in paragraphs 42-43 will apply from the date that the application for the administration, or the notice of intention to appoint, is filed at court. The interim moratorium does not stop certain specified actions.

674.   Paragraph 45 sets out that, while a company is in administration, every business document (e.g. invoices, orders for goods and services or business letters) issued by, or on behalf of, the company or the administrator must identify the administrator and state that the affairs, business and property of the company are being managed by him or her.

PROCESS OF ADMINISTRATION

675.   A diagram showing the process of administration is at Annex G.

676.   Paragraphs 46-48 provide that, in all cases, once the administrator has been appointed,

he or she will send notice of the appointment to the company and its creditors as soon as is reasonably practicable and send notice to the Registrar of Companies within seven days of the appointment. He or she will also require, by notice, a representative of the company (e.g. officer of the company, employee) to provide a statement of the company's affairs within eleven days of the notice being received. This statement must be verified by a statement of truth and give particulars of the company's property, debts and liabilities, and the details of each creditor and their security.

Administrator's proposals and meeting of creditors

677.   A diagram showing the conclusion of administration is at Annex H.

678.   Paragraph 49 provides that, as soon as reasonably practicable, or, in any event, within 8 weeks of the administration commencing, the administrator is required to make a statement setting out proposals for achieving the purpose of administration, although this period can be extended with the permission of the court or with the consent of the creditors (see paragraphs 107 and 108). The administrator will send a copy of the proposals to the Registrar of Companies, the company's creditors and every member of the company (the last obligation may be fulfilled by publishing a notice). In cases where the business of the company had to be sold under a short timescale to maximise the economic value, the administrator will report these facts to the creditors in his or her proposal.

679.   Each copy of the administrator's proposals sent to creditors must be accompanied by an invitation to an initial creditors' meeting, which must be held as soon as reasonably practicable, or, and in any event, within ten weeks of the administration commencing, and on a prescribed period of notice (paragraphs 50 and 51). The time periods may be extended with the permission of the court or the consent of creditors (see paragraphs 107 and 108). If the administrator does not consider that it is reasonably practicable to rescue the company and/or achieve a better result for the creditors than on a winding-up, his or her statement must state why (paragraph 49).

680.   The administrator's proposals will take into account the purpose of administration, i.e.:

    a)   to rescue the company as a going concern (paragraph 3(1)(a));

    b)   if that is not reasonably practicable, or would not yield the best outcome for creditors, to achieve a better result for the company's creditors as a whole than would have been achieved if the company were wound up (without first being in administration) (paragraph 3(1)(b));

    c)   if it is not reasonably practicable to achieve 3(1)(a) or 3(1)(b), to realise the company's property and make payments to preferential and secured creditors (paragraph 3(1)(c)).

681.   The administrator will present a copy of his or her proposals at the initial creditors'

meeting. If the administrator concludes that the company can be rescued as a going concern, he or she will put the proposal to the creditors and they will decide whether to accept an arrangement under which they will agree to accept less than full payment of their debts. This will usually be through a CVA or a scheme of arrangement under section 425 Companies Act 1985. The creditors could decide to reject the proposals or, with the consent of the administrator, amend them.

682.   If company rescue is not deemed reasonably practicable, or would not yield the best outcome for creditors, the administrator will explain why this is so, and put the proposal to the creditors setting out how he or she plans to achieve a better result for the company's creditors as a whole (e.g. as a result of selling the company's businesses as going concerns to one or more buyers). The creditors will vote on whether to accept, modify or reject the proposal.

683.   Where it is anticipated that there will be no funds available from the insolvent estate for unsecured creditors, outside those flowing from the abolition of Crown preference, the administrator will not be required to call a meeting of the creditors. This will also be the case where the administrator thinks there are funds to pay all creditors in full or that the first two objectives cannot be achieved. However, within the prescribed period, such a meeting may be requisitioned by creditors whose debts amount to at least 10% of the total debts of the company (paragraph 52).

684.   An administrator's statement of proposals may not include any proposal that affects the right of a secured creditor to enforce his or her security without his or her consent. In addition, the statement of proposals may not include any action that would result in a preferential debt being paid otherwise than in a priority to a non-preferential debt (paragraph 73).

685.   A creditors' meeting may only modify the administrator's proposals with his or her consent (paragraph 53). The administrator cannot subsequently make any substantial revisions to the proposals without first obtaining the agreement of the creditors (paragraph 54).

686.   After the conclusion of the initial creditors' meeting (and any subsequent meeting), the administrator will report any decision taken to the court and the registrar of companies. If the creditors fail to approve the proposals, the court may provide that the administrator's appointment shall cease to have effect, adjourn the hearing conditionally or unconditionally, make an interim order, make an order on a suspended petition for winding up, or any other order deemed appropriate (paragraph 55). Paragraph 57 makes provision for the establishment of a creditors' committee.

687.   Anything that is required to be done at or by a creditors' meeting may be done by correspondence, including communicating electronically and by telephone or fax (paragraphs 58 and 111).

Functions of the administrator

688.   Paragraph 59 provides that the administrator may do anything necessary or expedient for the management of the affairs, business and property of the company. Schedule 1 to the Insolvency Act 1986 sets out the powers of the administrator.

689.   Paragraph 61 provides that the administrator may remove or appoint a company director.

690.   An administrator may make a distribution to secured creditors and preferential creditors without permission of the court (paragraph 65). He or she may make distributions to unsecured creditors with the permission of the court. The administrator can make a payment if he or she thinks that the payment is likely to assist in achieving the purpose of administration or in accordance with paragraph 13 of Schedule 1 to the Insolvency Act 1986 (paragraph 66). On appointment, an administrator is required to take on custody or control of all the property to which he or she thinks the company is entitled (paragraph 67).

691.   Paragraph 70 provides that the administrator may dispose of property, subject to a floating charge (as created), as if the property were unencumbered, without the consent of the floating charge holder. However, the floating charge holder has first call on the proceeds of sale.

692.   Paragraph 71 provides that the court may give the administrator the power to override the rights of the holder of a fixed security over the company's property and the power to dispose of the property in question as if it were owned by the company. However, the holder of the fixed security has first call on the proceeds of sale.

693.   Paragraph 72 provides that the court may give the administrator the power to sell property subject to a hire-purchase agreement as if the property in question were owned by the company. However, the hire-purchase creditor has first call on the proceeds of sale.

Challenge to the administrator's conduct of the company

694.   Paragraph 74 provides that any creditor or member of a company in administration may apply to the court, firstly, if he or she believes that the administrator has acted, or proposes to act, in a way that could unfairly harm his or her interests. Secondly, if he or she believes that the administrator is not performing his or her functions as quickly and efficiently as is reasonably practicable. The use of the expression "reasonably practicable" conveys the idea that one administration may be very different from another, where it may be practicable to act within a short time in the administration of a simple, small company, that may be entirely impracticable in the case of a large complicated case. Furthermore the courts would be unlikely to entertain claims under this provision relating to trivial delays or that are frivolous or unavoidable or cause no

harm.

695. The court may grant relief, adjourn the hearing conditionally or unconditionally or make an interim or other order deemed appropriate. However, an order may not be made if it would impede or prevent the implementation of an approved voluntary arrangement or an arrangement sanctioned under section 425 Companies Act 1985, or proposals under paragraphs 53-54, where the challenge is made more than 28 days after the approval of those proposals.

Misfeasance

696. An interested party may apply to the court if he or she considers that the administrator has misapplied or retained the company's property, has become accountable for property, has committed a breach of a fiduciary, or other duty in relation to the company, or has been guilty of misfeasance. The court may order the administrator to repay, restore or account for the property, pay interest, or contribute by way of compensation to the company's property for breach of duty or misfeasance (paragraph 75).

Ending administration

697. The administrator will complete the administration as soon as reasonably practicable, or, in any event, within twelve months of the date the administration commenced. However, this term may be extended for an additional period of up to six months with the consent of creditors. Alternatively, the administrator can apply to court for an extension for as long as deemed necessary by the courts (paragraph 76 and 78). An extension may not be made not be made once the administrators term of office has ended (paragraph 77).

698. The administrator is required to apply to the court to end the appointment if he or she thinks that the purpose of administration cannot be achieved, that the company should not have entered into administration or if required to do so by a creditors' meeting (paragraph 79).

699. If the administrator thinks that the purpose of administration has been sufficiently achieved he or she will file notice with the court and the Registrar of Companies and send copies to all the company's creditors. The administrator's appointment will end when the notice is filed (paragraph 80). Paragraph 81 makes provision for a creditor to apply to the court to have an administration stopped if he or she considers that the appointment was made under an improper motive.

700. Paragraph 83 allows the administrator to end the administration and convert the proceedings into a voluntary winding-up. This will occur if the preferential and secured creditors have been paid all they are likely to receive (or such has been set aside for them), and there is money available for the unsecured creditors. The

administrator will send a notice to the Registrar of Companies and, as soon as is reasonably practicable, file a copy with the court and send a copy to each of the company's creditors. Once the Registrar of Companies has registered the notice, the administrator's appointment ends, the company proceeds to undergo a creditors' voluntary winding-up and the administrator becomes the liquidator of the company, unless the creditors have nominated an alternative liquidator.

Dissolution

701. Paragraph 84 provides that the administrator may take steps to dissolve the company where he or she finds that the company has no further assets to make a distribution to creditors. In which case he or she may send a notice to the Registrar of Companies and send a copy to the court and to each of the creditors. The company is considered dissolved after three months of the registration of the notice. However, it will be open to the court, on the application of the administrator or any other interested person, to defer the dissolution of the company; any such order should be filed with the Registrar of Companies.

Replacing administrator

702. Paragraphs 87-99 provide for the removal or replacement of the administrator under the different routes into administration and provide for release and priority of the administrator's debts and liabilities.

General provisions

703. Paragraphs 100 to 111 make general provisions relating to the appointment of joint and concurrent administrators (paragraph 100 to 103), matters of penalties (paragraph 106), time-limits (paragraph 107 to 110) and interpretation (paragraph (111).

704. Paragraphs 115 to 119 make provision for various issues of relevance to administration in Scotland, in particular, the interpretation of the expressions "filing in court" and "charge", the application of the provisions concerning the disposal of property subject to security and hire purchase agreements, and they provide an express order of priority.

705. Schedule 17 contains minor and consequential amendments arising out of the changes to administration.

Section 249: Special administration regimes
706. This section applies to companies for which special arrangements for the administration procedure have been made by applying Part II of the Insolvency Act 1986, with modifications. These special administration schemes are:

- water companies under the Water Industry Act 1991;

- companies to which railway administration orders apply (railway companies under the Railways Act 1993 and companies involved in the Channel Tunnel Rail Link);

- air traffic control companies under the Transport Act 2000;

- London Underground PPP companies under the Greater London Authority Act 1999; and

- building societies as defined by the Building Societies Act 1986.

707. The section provides an automatic saving provision for Part II as it is presently applied and modified by the various enactments listed above to continue to apply to companies subject to these regimes.

708. It also allows the Secretary of State (or HM Treasury in the case of building societies), by order, to amend the existing provisions in Part II (and to make consequential amendments of other enactments) as they are applied to the special regimes.

Section 250 & Schedule 18: Prohibition of appointment of administrative receiver & Schedule 2A to Insolvency Act 1986

709. This section inserts a new Chapter IV after Chapter III of Part III of the Insolvency Act 1986. Schedule 18 introduces new Schedule 2A to the Insolvency Act 1986 (inserted after Schedule 2).

710. Currently, a floating charge holder, whose security covers the whole or substantially the whole of the company's property, may enforce their contractual right to realise their security by appointing an AR (often simply referred to as a receiver in Scotland). In order to restrict the use of administrative receivership, new section 72A of Chapter IV prohibits, subject to certain exceptions, the holder of a qualifying floating charge (as defined under paragraph 14 of Schedule B1) from appointing an AR. The section applies to any floating charge created on or after the date that it comes into force.

711. However, there are cases where administrative receivership plays a crucial role. These exceptions to section 72A are set out in sections 72B-72G.

712. Section 72B provides that an AR can be appointed in pursuance of an arrangement which is, or forms part of, a capital market arrangement (as defined by paragraph 1 of Schedule 2A of Insolvency Act 1986 – see section 250 and Schedule 18), i.e.:

- it involves security that has been granted to a person holding a capital market investment issued by a party to the arrangement; or

- at least one party to the arrangement guarantees the performance of the obligations of another party; or

- at least one party provides security in respect of the performance of the obligations of another party; or

- the arrangement involves the issue of options, futures or contracts for differences.

713.   This only applies if the debt, or expected debt, is at least £50 million and involves the issue of capital market investments as defined by paragraphs 2 and 3 of new Schedule 2A to the Insolvency Act 1986 (paragraph 1(1) of Schedule 18).

714.   Section 72C provides that an AR can be appointed in respect of the property of a project company of a public-private partnership (PPP) project with step-in rights:

- a PPP project is one whose resources are provided partly by one or more public bodies and partly by one or more private bodies; or which is designed wholly or mainly to assist a public body in discharging a function.

- a project has 'step-in rights' if the person who provides finance (including an indemnity) for the project has a conditional right that enables them to assume sole or principal contractual responsibility for carrying out all or part of the project or to make payments so to do.

715.   Section 72D provides that an AR can be appointed if the floating charge is granted over the property of a project company of a utility project with step-in rights.

716.   A utility project is a project designed wholly or mainly for the purpose of a regulated business (e.g. a project that is concerned with a business carried out requiring a licence granted under section 8 Railways Act 1993, or a licence granted under section 7A Gas Act 1986). A full list of such regulated businesses is given in paragraph 10 of Schedule 18.

717.   Section 72E provides that an AR can be appointed in respect of an arrangement in relation to a project company of a financed project with step-in rights. This only applies if the project company incurs a debt of at least £50 million for the purposes of carrying out the project.

718.   Section 72F provides that an AR can be appointed by someone entitled to do so in connection with a market charge within the meaning of the Companies Act 1989; a system-charge within the meaning of the Financial Markets and Insolvency Regulations 1996; and a collateral security charge within the meaning of the Financial

Markets and Insolvency (Settlement Finality) Regulations 1999.

719.   Section 72G provides that an AR can be appointed if the floating charge is granted over a company which is registered as a social landlord under Part I of the Housing Act 1996 or Part 3 of the Housing (Scotland) Act 2001.

720.   Section 72H inserts what will be new Schedule 2A into the Insolvency Act 1986, after the existing Schedule 2. It also gives the Secretary of State the power to amend the new provisions in Chapter IV to Part III of the Act. Specifically, the Secretary of State may, by order:

- insert additional exceptions to new section 72A;

- provide that an exception already provided for shall cease to have effect;

- amend section 72A in consequence of any new exception (or removal thereof);

- amend any of the exceptions 72B-72G;

- amend Schedule 2A.

Sections 251 and 252: Abolition of Crown Preference & Unsecured creditors

721.   The White Paper *'Productivity and Enterprise: Insolvency – A Second Chance'* made a commitment to abolish the Crown's preferential status in insolvency, and to ensure that the benefit went to unsecured creditors for companies that have given floating-charges after the provision has come into force.

722.   As a preferential creditor, the Crown can currently claim its debts from an insolvent company or bankrupt estate ahead of secured creditors, who hold a floating charge, and unsecured creditors. The Crown's preferential debts are described in sections 386 and 387 of, and Schedule 6 to, the Insolvency Act 1986, and include arrears of PAYE, NIC, and VAT for the following periods:

- debts due to the Inland Revenue for 12 months prior to the relevant date (category 1 of Schedule 6);

- debts due to Customs and Excise for the 6 to 12 months prior to the relevant date (category 2 of Schedule 6);

- social security contributions for the 12 months prior to the relevant date (category 3 of Schedule 6)..

723.   The Act will abolish the Crown's preferential status.

724.   The relevant date is defined by section 387 Insolvency Act 1986.

725.   Preferential status will remain for:

*   contributions to occupational pension schemes (category 4);

*   remuneration of employees for the relevant period (category 5); and

*   levies on coal and steel production under the European Coal and Steel Community (ECSC) Treaty.

726.   In addition, Schedule 17 removes section 189(4) of the Employment Rights Act 1996. As a result, the Secretary of State will no longer be paid in priority to any remaining preferential claims lodged in the insolvency proceedings by former employees. The Secretary of State will remain a preferential creditor where he has "stepped into an employee's shoes" and made payments from the National Insurance Fund to cover all or part of any employee's preferential claims.

Section 251: Abolition of Crown Preference

727.   Section 251 *subsection (1)* removes paragraphs 1 and 2 (debts due to Inland Revenue), paragraphs 3-5C (debts due to Customs and Excise), and paragraphs 6 and 7 (social security contributions) from Schedule 6 to the Insolvency Act 1986, putting into effect the abolition of Crown preference. Subsection (2) makes similar changes for Scotland.

Section 252: Unsecured creditors

728.   This section inserts a new section 176A (Share of assets for unsecured creditors) after section 176 of the Insolvency Act 1986. Section 176A provides for a prescribed part (a percentage share of the company's net property (as defined)) to go to unsecured creditors, although the percentage itself will be prescribed by Statutory Instrument (*subsections (7)-(8)*), the setting of which percentage will be subject to consultation.

729.   Where a company has gone into liquidation, administration, provisional liquidation or receivership, the office-holder will make part of the company's net property available to unsecured creditors (i.e. after taking into account any preferential debts, any liability subject to a fixed charge and the costs of realising the company's property). However, it will not be necessary for the office-holder to distribute funds to unsecured creditors if they are less than the prescribed minimum, and he or she thinks that the cost of making a distribution would be disproportionate to the benefits. Where the prescribed part is greater than or equal to the minimum, but the costs of distribution are disproportionate to the benefits, the office holder will be able to apply to the court to waive the requirement.

Sanction of actions in relation to antecedent recoveries

Sections 253 and 262: Liquidator's powers & Powers of trustee in bankruptcy

730.   The Insolvency Act 1986 contains measures to enable liquidators and trustees in bankruptcy to take legal action to seek financial restitution for losses caused to the insolvent estate. The provisions providing for the actions in question are: sections 213 (fraudulent trading); 214 (wrongful trading); 238 (transactions at an undervalue – corporate); 239 (preferences – corporate); 242 (gratuitous alienations – Scotland); 243 (unfair preferences – Scotland); 339 (transactions at an undervalue – bankruptcy); 340 (preferences – bankruptcy) and 423 (transactions defrauding creditors).

731.   These sections provide that the liquidator (section 253), or trustee in bankruptcy (section 262) must have sanction (i.e. approval), usually of the creditors or the court, before taking such antecedent recovery action.

Section 254: Application of insolvency law to foreign company

732.   This section will allow, for example, the Secretary of State to apply the rescue provisions of the Insolvency Act 1986 to foreign incorporated companies through detailed secondary legislation. Part V of the Insolvency Act 1986 allows unregistered companies to be wound up by the court, such companies include foreign registered companies. Once this secondary legislation has been approved then such companies (particularly those with assets, creditors and employees in this country) will be able to make use of the rescue provisions, whereas currently the only option available is to be wound up by the court as an unregistered company.

Section 255: Application of law about company arrangement or administration to non-company

733.   This section allows HM Treasury, with the concurrence of the Secretary of State, to make an order to provide for company arrangement and administration provisions to apply to certain non-companies, namely industrial and provident societies and friendly societies. This will enable the Government to apply those insolvency procedures, with any modifications that are necessary, to some or all of these societies through secondary legislation. The power will not be exercised without full consultation with all interested parties. The order may not apply in relation to a society which is registered as a social landlord under Part I of the Housing Act 1996 or Part 3 of the Housing (Scotland) Act 2001.

Individuals

Sections 256 and 269 & Schedules 19 and 23: Duration of bankruptcy & Minor and consequential amendments

734.   Currently, bankrupts are discharged from bankruptcy three years after the making of the bankruptcy order, although there are exceptions to this rule; for example: in cases where the court has made an order for summary administration; where the bankrupt does not comply with his or her obligations and the court suspends automatic discharge; and where the debtor has been an undischarged bankrupt within the previous fifteen years or remains subject to an existing criminal bankruptcy order. However, in general, the duration of the bankruptcy is the same for bankrupts

regardless of culpability or the level of their assets or liabilities.

735. Section 256 replaces the existing section 279 Insolvency Act 1986 on duration of bankruptcy. It provides for bankrupts to be automatically discharged one year after the bankruptcy order was made, but the period may be reduced if the Official Receiver files a notice stating that further investigation into the bankrupt's conduct and affairs is unnecessary, or has been concluded. The ability to suspend discharge where the bankrupt fails to comply with an obligation remains (see new subsections (3) and (4)). At present, where a bankruptcy order is made upon a debtor's own petition and, at that time, the debt is less than the small bankruptcies level (currently £20,000), and in the preceding five years the debtor has not been made bankrupt or entered into an individual voluntary arrangement, the court may issue a certificate of summary administration. One of the effects of this certificate is to reduce the discharge period from three to two years.

736. In order to reduce the discharge period to one year, it will be necessary to make amendments to current bankruptcy legislation, for example repealing those provisions in the Insolvency Act 1986 dealing with summary administration. These amendments are made in Schedule 23 to the Act, which is given effect by section 269.

737. As the discharge period is being altered, transitional provision needs to be made to deal with individuals who have already been made bankrupt on commencement but have not yet been discharged. This is done in Schedule 19. In this case, neither the existing nor the new section 279 Insolvency Act 1986 will apply. Instead, Schedule 19 provides that the date of discharge will be one year from the date of commencement of section 256 or earlier if the three-year discharge period is due to end before that date.

738. The position is different for those individuals who have been undischarged bankrupts more than once in the previous fifteen years and who are still undischarged at the time section 256 commences. In this case, the bankrupt is discharged five years from the date of commencement or earlier if an order under section 280(2) Insolvency Act 1986 is made or comes into effect. Section 280(2) allows the court to refuse discharge, conditionally discharge or absolutely discharge a bankrupt on his or her application. An application can be made any time after five years from the date of bankruptcy so that, for example, a person made bankrupt for the second time one year before the date of commencement of section 256 would be eligible to apply for discharge under section 280 four years after. If the court grants discharge on such an application, it will have effect from that date. If he or she makes no such application, or an application is refused, discharge will occur automatically five years after commencement.

739. Those persons made bankrupt under section 264(1)(d) (criminal bankruptcy) can only be discharged by order of the court under section 280 Insolvency Act 1986.

Sections 257 and 263 & Schedules 20 and 21: Post-discharge restrictions &

Repeal of certain bankruptcy offences

740.   The provisions of the Act remove some of the unnecessary restrictions that automatically apply as a result of bankruptcy (such as disqualification from holding certain offices (see further notes on sections 265, 266, 267 and 268)) and repeal two offences (section 263).

741.   They also provide protection to the public and business community against the minority of bankrupts who abuse the system or whose conduct has been dishonest or otherwise culpable, either before or after bankruptcy. The Act introduces bankruptcy restrictions orders (BROs) that will have the effect of imposing restrictions on such bankrupts. BROs will run for a minimum period of two years and a maximum of fifteen years.

742.   These restrictions are currently only triggered by the existence of a bankruptcy order (such as the obligation to declare your status as an undischarged bankrupt when obtaining credit of more than £250 (section 360(1) of insolvency legislation and the Insolvency Proceedings (Monetary Limits) Order 1986). By amending the discharge period, these restrictions will fall away for non-culpable bankrupts after a maximum of one year. Schedule 21 amends those provisions of the Insolvency Act 1986 that contain restrictions by adding references to BROs and interim BROs. These include section 31, which makes it an offence for a person to act as receiver or manager of a company's property if he or she is an undischarged bankrupt. In this way, such restrictions will continue to apply to persons whose bankruptcy has been discharged but who are subject to a BRO.

743.   Schedule 20 inserts a new Schedule 4A into the Insolvency Act 1986 that sets out the details regarding BROs and bankruptcy restrictions undertakings (BRUs). BROs are made by the court on the application of the Secretary of State or the Official Receiver acting on the direction of the Secretary of State (paragraph 1 of new Schedule 4A).

744.   Under paragraphs 7-9 of new Schedule 4A any reference to a person against whom a BRO has been made includes a reference to a person who is the subject of a BRU (paragraph 8). This will allow the bankrupt to agree to be bound by such restrictions without the need for an application to court. The minimum and maximum duration of a BRU will be the same as a BRO.

745.   Paragraph 2 of Schedule 4A sets out the kinds of conduct to which the court will have particular regard in making a BRO. Failure to keep proper accounting records, and gambling and rash and hazardous speculation are types of conduct already covered by criminal offences in sections 361 and 362 Insolvency Act 1986. Section 263 repeals those two offences. In future, matters that would have been dealt with under those two offences will, provided the misconduct is material having regard to the circumstances of the case, be dealt with under the new bankruptcy restrictions regime.

746.   Paragraph 3 provides that an application for a BRO must be made within one year of the making of the bankruptcy order. It also provides that proceedings may be brought

outside this time scale but only with the permission of the court. The order will come into force when it is made and will last until the date specified in the order, which will be a minimum of two years and a maximum of fifteen years (paragraph 4).

747. It is unlikely in many cases that a substantive decision will be made by the court in relation to an application for a BRO before the defendant's discharge. Thus, there is likely to be a gap in time between the discharge of the bankrupt and the making of the BRO in those cases where a BRO is being sought. Paragraphs 5 and 6 make provision for the court to make an interim order that can be made when issuing proceedings. The court may make an interim BRO where the Official Receiver or Secretary of State has made out a *prima facie* case and the court is of the view that the misconduct is so serious that it is in the public interest to make such an order. The restrictions then apply on the making of the interim order, by virtue of paragraph 5(4).

748. Paragraphs 10 and 11 set out the effects of annulment of the bankruptcy on any BRO. Where a bankruptcy order is annulled under section 282(1)(a) Insolvency Act 1986 on the grounds that it ought not have been made, any BRO, either substantive or interim, that is in force will be annulled.

749. A bankruptcy order annulled because an individual voluntary arrangement has been approved by the creditors (sections 261 and 263D of the Insolvency Act 1986), or because the bankruptcy debts and expenses have been paid in full, will not affect whether a BRO or interim order remains in force. Where an application has been made, then those proceedings can be continued notwithstanding the annulment of the bankruptcy. This permits the making of BROs against culpable bankrupts who have managed to have their bankruptcy order annulled solely because they are now able, for whatever reason, to pay off their debts either in full or partially to the satisfaction of their creditors. Where a BRU has been offered, the undertaking can be finalised notwithstanding any annulment under sections 261 and 263D Insolvency Act 1986.

750. Paragraph 12 requires the Secretary of State to maintain a public register of BROs, interim BROs and BRUs. Paragraph 16 of Schedule 23 inserts a new paragraph 29A into Schedule 9 of the Insolvency Act 1986. This allows, amongst other things, Rules to be made about the inspection of the register.

751. Schedule 21 deals with the effect of BROs, interim BROs and BRUs. It amends certain provisions that make particular conduct an offence while an undischarged bankrupt and extends them to cover individuals subject to BROs, interim BROs and BRUs (incorporated by virtue of paragraphs 5(4) and 8 of new Schedule 4A of the Insolvency Act 1986 respectively). The conduct includes:

- acting as receiver or manager of a company's property on behalf of a debenture holder (section 31 Insolvency Act 1986);

- obtaining credit above the prescribed limit without disclosing that you are the subject of a Bankruptcy Restrictions Order (section 360 Insolvency Act 1986);

- trading in a name other than that under which a person was made bankrupt (section 360 Insolvency Act 1986);

- disqualification from acting as an insolvency practitioner (section 390 Insolvency Act 1986); and

- disqualification from acting as a company director (section 11(1) CDDA1986).

752. Section 350(3) of the Insolvency Act 1986 limits the liability of a bankrupt for offences under Part VI of that Act to acts committed prior to his discharge. Paragraph 2 of Schedule 21 qualifies that provision so that a person subject to a BRO who commits an offence extended to BROs after discharge can still be prosecuted.

Section 258: Investigation by official receiver

753. Currently, under section 289 Insolvency Act 1986, there is a duty on the Official Receiver to investigate the conduct and affairs of every bankrupt and to make any report to the court that he or she thinks fit, except in summary cases when the Official Receiver will only investigate if he or she deems it necessary. This distinction is made on the basis that cases with relatively small unsecured liabilities (summary cases with unsecured liabilities of less than £20,000 – often consumer bankruptcies) do not require as extensive a use of the Official Receiver's resources as those involving large debts with greater losses to the creditors. However, there are cases where the bankrupt's debts are large (for example, where the liabilities of a limited company are guaranteed) in which no investigation is required or some small, yet complex, cases that require extensive investigation.

754. Section 258 inserts a new section 289 into the Insolvency Act 1986 that removes this automatic obligation to investigate every case and provides that the Official Receiver is only required to investigate the conduct and affairs of any bankrupt where he or she think it necessary). *Subsections (3) and (4)* of the new provision merely re-enact the old section 289(2) and (3).

Sections 259 and 260: Income payments order & Income payments agreement

755. The current income payments order regime is designed to ensure bankrupts make an affordable contribution towards their debt from their income for up to three years, but in most cases they cease on discharge (see section 310(6)). Against the background of a reduced period of bankruptcy for non-culpable bankrupts, income payments orders will now last for a term of up to three years from the date of the order, irrespective of discharge (see new section 310(6) inserted by section 259).

756. Income payments orders are made by the courts on the application of the trustee in bankruptcy. In practice most are not usually contested. Income payments orders can

be varied on the application of the trustee or the bankrupt.

757.   In order to remove the need for court involvement in non-contentious cases, section 260 introduces the concept of the income payments agreement by inserting a new Section 310A into the Insolvency Act 1986.

758.   Income payments agreements will provide a legally-binding written agreement between the bankrupt and the Official Receiver or trustee that requires the bankrupt (or a third party) to make specified payments to his trustee for a specified period. This will be enforceable as if it were an income payments order made by the court. Whilst in force, an income payments agreement may be varied on an application to the court by the bankrupt, trustee or the Official Receiver or by written agreement between the parties. A court may not vary an income payments agreement to include a provision that could not be included in an income payments order and must grant a variation if it takes the view that the variation is necessary to enable the bankrupt to retain sufficient funds to meet the reasonable domestic needs of the bankrupt and his or her family.

759.   An income payments agreement must specify the period in which it is to have effect and that period can apply after a bankrupt is discharged but cannot extend to a date more than three years after the date of the income payments agreement.

760.   Paragraph 7 of Schedule 19 sets out the transitional provisions as they relate to income payments orders in existence at the time of commencement.

Section 261: Bankrupt's Home

761.   Section 261 makes provision in relation to the sole or principal residence of the bankrupt, the bankrupt's spouse or the former spouse of a bankrupt, and where the bankrupt has an interest that is comprised in the bankrupt's estate. The section (*subsection (1)*) inserts section 283A into the Insolvency Act 1986. This new section provides that where a bankrupt's estate comprises an interest in such a residence, that interest reverts back to the bankrupt unless within the three year period following the date of the bankruptcy the trustee:

(a) realises the interest;

(b) applies for an order of sale or possession in respect of the premises in which the interest subsists;

(c) applies for a charging order over the premises in respect of the value of the interest; or

(d) enters into an agreement with the bankrupt regarding the interest.

762.   The section (*subsection (3)*) also inserts a new section 313A into the Insolvency Act 1986 which provides for the dismissal of applications for orders for sale, possession

or a charging order in respect of the bankrupt's residence where the value of the bankrupt's interest is below a level prescribed in secondary legislation.

Section 264 & Schedule 22: Individual voluntary arrangement

763.   Individual voluntary arrangements are an alternative to bankruptcy, without the same automatic restrictions, where the debtor comes to an arrangement with his or her creditors about the repayment of his or her debts. They generally provide a better return to creditors. Currently there are around 7,000 individual voluntary arrangements made each year, of which a very small minority are entered into after a bankruptcy order has been made.

764.   At present, a debtor can make a proposal for an individual voluntary arrangement (see Part VIII of the Insolvency Act 1986). Those proposals also put forward a person to supervise the implementation of that arrangement, the nominee (on approval of an arrangement the nominee becomes supervisor). To act as the nominee (from 1 January 2003, as a result of the relevant amendments introduced by the Insolvency Act 2000) or supervisor, a person must be a qualified insolvency practitioner. In practice, the debtor sends the nominee a copy of the proposal and a statement of his or her affairs. He or she can then apply for an interim order that has the effect of staying any actions against them or their property (see sections 252–255 of the Insolvency Act 1986). The nominee reports to the court, stating whether a meeting of creditors should be called to consider the proposal. If a meeting is called and the creditors approve the individual voluntary arrangement, the interim order can be discharged and any bankruptcy order may be annulled. Modifications can be made to the proposal if the debtor so consents.

765.   In order to encourage greater use of individual voluntary arrangements, this section makes two changes to the current individual voluntary arrangements regime.

766.   First, it enables Official Receivers to act as nominees and supervisors for post-bankruptcy individual voluntary arrangements (see paragraph 3 of Schedule 22, which inserts a new Section 389B into the Insolvency Act 1986). This provides debtors and creditors with a choice of who should administer the arrangement: either a private sector insolvency practitioner or an Official Receiver. There is also an order-making power to extend the ability for the Official Receiver to act as nominee and supervisor to all cases.

767.   Second, it introduces a new fast-track scheme for post-bankruptcy individual voluntary arrangements where the Official Receiver is the proposed nominee (see paragraph 2 of Schedule 22, which inserts a new section 263A – 263G into the Insolvency Act 1986). Under this regime, the proposal will be agreed with the Official Receiver and filed with the Court. No meeting of the creditors will be called and it will not be possible to modify the proposal. The Official Receiver will send out the proposal to the creditors on a 'take it or leave it' basis and the creditors will either agree to or disagree with the proposal by correspondence. If the individual voluntary arrangement is approved, the Official Receiver will notify the court and the court can

then annul the bankruptcy order. It is proposed that the majority required for approval will remain unchanged (the provision on majority is set out in Rule 5.18 of the Insolvency Rules 1986 (SI1986/1925)), which majority is three quarters in value. From 1 January 2003, as a result of changes introduced by SI 2002/2712, that provision will be found at Rule 5.23.

Sections 265, 266, 267 and 268: Disqualification from office: Justice of the Peace, Parliament, Local government & General

768. Currently bankrupts are subject to a wide range of statutory restrictions, prohibitions or disqualifications irrespective of the level of their assets and liabilities, or culpability. These restrictions prevent the bankrupt from being elected to or holding specified positions or offices, or becoming or remaining a member of specified bodies or groups. Generally, these restrictions are in place for the duration of the bankruptcy (currently three years in most cases). While in some cases these restrictions can be justified in the public interest, there is little justification for others (e.g. serving as a Justice of the Peace or member of a Local Authority).

Section 266: Disqualification from office: Parliament

769. Section 427 of the Insolvency Act 1986 imposes a number of restrictions on a member of either House at Westminster if he or she is adjudged bankrupt (or sequestrated in Scotland). In the House of Lords, a member is not allowed to sit or vote in either the House or Committee. In the Commons, a member cannot be elected to, sit or vote in the House (or the devolved equivalent) or on Committee. The restrictions on being elected to and sitting and voting in the devolved assemblies on the ground of bankruptcy feed through from section 427 by virtue of the Government of Wales Act 1998, the Scotland Act 1998 and the Northern Ireland Act 1998.

770. With the exception of a peer in Westminster, in all legislatures a bankrupt is given six months in order to have their bankruptcy order annulled or their bankruptcy discharged. If this has not happened by the end of that period, then their seat is vacated.

771. Section 266 inserts new sections into the Insolvency Act 1986 to deal with disqualification from Parliament, the Scottish Parliament, the Northern Ireland Assembly or the National Assembly for Wales where a BRO is made against a member of any of those Assemblies. It also amends section 427 Insolvency Act 1986 to remove references to England and Wales from that section and to change its title.

England and Wales

772. The new section 426A disqualifies an MP against whom a BRO is made from membership of the House of Commons. On disqualification under this section, an MP must immediately vacate his or her seat. This differs from the current position under section 427 Insolvency Act 1986, which disqualifies a person on the making of a bankruptcy order but then gives a period of six months for an MP to have the bankruptcy order annulled. Under the new section, an MP is no longer automatically disqualified on the making of a bankruptcy order. Those MPs where some form of

culpability can be shown through the making of a BRO will be disqualified automatically and there will be no six months grace period.

773. A member of the House of Lords subject to a BRO will be disqualified from sitting or voting in the House of Lords or from sitting or voting in a committee of the House of Lords or a joint committee of both Houses. No writ of summons can be issued to a lord of Parliament who is subject to a BRO. These are the same restrictions as are currently in place for a bankruptcy order but, again, by replacing bankruptcy with BRO as the trigger to disqualification, only culpable peers will be disqualified.

The Devolved Assemblies

774. The new section 426A will feed through to the devolved Assemblies by virtue of the devolution legislation. A member of the Scottish Parliament against whom a BRO is made will be disqualified from the Scottish Parliament by virtue of section 15(1)(b) Scotland Act 1998 and will have to vacate his or her seat under sections 17(1) and (2) of that Act.

775. The position is the same for a member of the National Assembly for Wales by virtue of sections 12(2) and 14(1) and (2) Government of Wales Act 1998 and for a member of the Northern Ireland Assembly by virtue of sections 36(4) and 37(1) Northern Ireland Act 1998 and Article 370 of the Insolvency (Northern Ireland) Order 1989.

MPs, Peers and Members of the Devolved Assemblies made bankrupt in Northern Ireland or sequestrated in Scotland

776. There is no equivalent regime to BROs in either Scotland or Northern Ireland. Insolvency law in Wales is the same as in England and will be modified by this Act.

777. Therefore, the existing regime for disqualification where an MP, peer or a member of a devolved Assembly is made bankrupt in Northern Ireland or sequestrated in Scotland is being retained. However, section 427 is being amended by section 266(1) and (2) so that it will then only cover those made bankrupt in Northern Ireland or sequestrated in Scotland.

778. For example, an MSP who is sequestrated in Scotland will be disqualified and will have six months to have that order annulled before having to vacate his or her seat.

Two regimes

779. Therefore, two different regimes will be in operation at the same time in Parliament and all the devolved Assemblies, depending on the jurisdiction in which the bankruptcy occurs:

- where a member of Parliament or a member of the devolved Assemblies is made bankrupt in England and Wales, these persons will not be automatically disqualified. Disqualification will be triggered if a BRO is made against him or her and he or she will have to vacate their seat immediately. A peer will be disqualified on the making of a BRO order from sitting and voting in the House of Lords or in Committee;

- where a member of Parliament or a member of the devolved Assemblies is made bankrupt in Northern Ireland or sequestrated in Scotland, they will be automatically disqualified on being made bankrupt or sequestrated and will have six months to have the order annulled. A peer who is a member of a devolved Assembly would be disqualified from the devolved Assembly and have six months to have the order annulled or his or her bankruptcy discharged and would be disqualified in Westminster from sitting and voting in the House of Lords or in Committee.

The order-making power

780. Section 266 provides for an order-making power to amend sections 426A and 426B, should equivalent regimes be introduced in Northern Ireland and Scotland. The order-making power would be subject to affirmative resolution.

781. Section 265 will remove the automatic disqualification on a bankrupt acting as a justice of the peace. The removal of bankrupt justices of the peace will be left to the Lord Chancellor's general power to appoint and remove justices of the peace where it is thought appropriate.

782. Section 267 will replace the automatic restriction on bankrupts serving as a member of a Local Authority with one disqualifying those subject to a BRO.

783. Section 268 will provide a wide order-making power for any Secretary of State or the National Assembly for Wales, to review legislation under his or her policy control and to maintain, repeal, amend or abolish such restrictions on bankrupts as they deem appropriate. Amendments can include reducing the class of bankrupts to whom a disqualification applies, applying the restrictions to those people who are subject to BROs or undertakings as well as bankrupts or providing that the disqualification is subject to the discretion of a specified person, body or group. Such orders will be subject to affirmative resolution.

Section 269 & Schedule 23: Minor and consequential amendments

784. Section 269 gives effect to Schedule 23, which makes minor and consequential amendments to the Insolvency Act 1986 as a result of the changes being made in the Act. Some of these amendments, such as those made because of the removal of summary bankruptcy, have been mentioned elsewhere. Paragraph 14 reflects the fact that the Official Receiver can act as a nominee and supervisor in an individual voluntary arrangement. Therefore the appointment provisions for Official Receivers in section 399 and the rules-making provisions in Schedule 23 have been amended accordingly.

785. Paragraph 12 extends the offence of concealment of property to section 354 Insolvency Act 1986 to include any failure to account for the loss of any substantial

property to the trustee. Currently, the provisions in section 354(3) set out the scope of the offence of a bankrupt failing – without reasonable excuse – either to account to the Official Receiver or the court for substantial losses or give satisfactory explanation for how such a loss came about. However, the realisation of assets is often administered by a trustee other than the Official Receiver.

786. Paragraph 13 adds subsections (4) and (5) to section 355 (concealment and falsification of accounting records) Insolvency Act 1986. The current provisions of section 355(2) and (3) detail offences relating to bankrupts who destroy, conceal, alter or dispose of books, papers or records in the twelve months prior to a bankruptcy petition being presented, or between the petition and order. In the case of 'trading records', that period is extended to two years (section 361 of the Insolvency Act 1986). The Act also repeals the current provisions of section 361, which will be dealt with by the new bankruptcy restrictions regime. As the availability of adequate records is crucial to the examination of the bankrupt's estates and enquiries into the bankrupt's affairs, subsection (4) extends the period from twelve months to two years. Subsection (5) provides a definition of the term 'trading record'.

787. County Court Administration Orders ('CCAOs') are made in the county courts and fall outside the insolvency regime. They are mechanisms for dealing with individuals with multiple debts and give the debtor respite from enforcement proceedings while they pay off their debts. Only those who have a county court judgment against them, at least one other debt, and total debts of less than £5,000, can apply for a CCAO. Currently, section 429 Insolvency Act 1986 allows a court to make an order placing restrictions on acquiring credit and the use of a trading name for up to two years where a debtor has failed to pay under a CCAO. Paragraph 15 amends section 429 County Courts Act 1984 to reflect the fact that restrictions flowing from the making of a bankruptcy order will only be for one year following the change to the discharge period. Therefore restrictions flowing from a CCAO will be similarly limited.

Money

788. The current financial regime of The Insolvency Service comprises numerous fees (see the Insolvency Fees Order 1986) covering case administration and a Secretary of State Fee, none of which achieves full cost recovery of activities undertaken by The Service. In addition, because of the low rate of interest set for estate balances invested in the Insolvency Services Investment Account, the amount returned to estates is considerably less than the level of investment income received by the account. The excess income is currently paid into the Consolidated Fund and amounted to some £43 million in 2000-01.

789. The Government has announced its intention to reform the regime to make it simpler and more transparent. It is also proposed to make the regime fairer to creditors, for example by returning to insolvent estates those investment returns that currently flow into the Consolidated Fund. The majority of the changes necessary to achieve reform will be made by using existing powers and changes to secondary legislation and

Rules. However, there are two specific areas that require primary legislation, and provisions for these are included in the Act.

Section 270: Fees

790. Section 270 *subsection (1)* inserts a new section 415A into the Insolvency Act 1986.

791. The new section will enable the Secretary of State to charge a fee to bodies recognised under section 391 Insolvency Act 1986 as a professional body for the purposes of licensing insolvency practitioners (IPs). It is intended that fees prescribed under this provision not only cover the cost of recognition but also the cost of monitoring the bodies' activities, such as overseeing their procedures and ensuring that licensing is carried out properly. The fee will also cover the cost of more general regulatory functions carried out by The Insolvency Service, such as representation on the Joint Insolvency Council and keeping IPs informed of legislative and other developments through the issuing of newsletters and guidance. The cost of these regulatory functions is currently met by the DTI but the new policy is that they should fall to the profession. The fee, which will be set out in secondary legislation, will be charged to each body based on the number of IPs licensed by them.

792. Subsection (2) of new section 415A provides for a fee to be charged to those IPs licensed by the Secretary of State under section 392, and will be based on the cost of granting and maintaining authorisation. The fee will also include the cost of monitoring the IP and the general regulatory functions undertaken by The Insolvency Service. As with the fee for the recognised bodies, the fee for IPs licensed by the Secretary of State will be set through secondary legislation. The level of the authorisation element of the fee will reflect more closely that charged by the recognised bodies to those IPs they license than the current authorisation fee of £100, which was set in 1986.

793. Subsection (3) provides for payment of fees that relate to the operation of the Insolvency Services Account by The Insolvency Service and money paid into or out of the Account. The Insolvency Service will separate out the costs that relate to its operation of the Insolvency Service Account so that these costs are met by insolvent estates. This will allow for clear identification of those banking services that are carried out in respect of all cases, and that will be charged through an annual service fee, and those that relate to specific estates and transactions such as investment requests by IPs or the volume of payments out of the account through cheques or bank transfers. These changes will also enable the ending of the current arrangements whereby a number of different fees are used to meet these costs and to cross-subsidise other functions. Subsection (4) applies the conditions that apply to fees under section 414 to those introduced under 415A.

Sections 271 and 272: Insolvency Services Account: interest & Insolvency Services Accounts

794. Section 405 of the Insolvency Act 1986 requires that any excess in investment income from the Insolvency Service Investment Account after payments to insolvent estates

and tax should be paid into the Consolidated Fund. Schedule 8 paragraph 16 and Schedule 9 paragraph 21 of the Insolvency Act 1986 enables the interest rate for the return of investment income to insolvent estates to be set through secondary legislation. The current rate of 3.5% has applied to companies since before the implementation of the 1986 Act. The Insolvency Act 2000 provided for payment of interest into bankruptcy estates.

795.   Section 271 introduces additions to Schedules 8 and 9 to the Insolvency Act 1986 to allow Rules to be made providing for the interest rate to be set by the Secretary of State by the issuing of a Notice, as opposed to through secondary legislation. This will enable the rate to be reviewed at regular intervals, probably annually, and allow changes in investment returns to the Account to flow through to insolvent estates without having to make regular amendments through statutory instruments.

796.   Section 272 *subsection (1)* removes the requirement under section 405 Insolvency Act 1986 for excess income from the Insolvency Services Investment Account to be paid into the Consolidated Fund.

797.   Section 408 of the Insolvency Act 1986 provides for recourse to the Consolidated Fund where, after payments received from the Investment Account, the Insolvency Services Account has insufficient funds to meet its liabilities. *Subsection (2)* of section 272 substitutes for the current section 408 a new section that incorporates the circumstances covered by the current section 408 and section 405 but provides wider powers that allow for adjustments to be made between the Insolvency Services Account or the Insolvency Services Investment Account and the Consolidated Fund. Adjustments may be necessary due to short-term fluctuations between the expected income, based on the level at which the interest rates are set and the actual investment return. This is because interest rates are set in advance, whereas the Investment Account is made up of investments purchased at different times, for different amounts, with differing returns and over different periods. New section 408 will enable the maintenance of a 'buffer' in the account to deal with such fluctuations and there may be occasions where adjustments need to be made between the account and the Consolidated Fund.

PART 11: SUPPLEMENTARY

Section 274: Provision of financial assistance for consumer purposes
798.   This section confirms the Secretary of State's powers to fund a wide range of activities that benefit consumers, including funding bodies such as the National Consumer Council and National Association of Citizens Advice Bureaux.

Sections 275, 276, 277, 278, 279, 280 and 281: Financial provision, Transitional or transitory provision and savings, Power to make consequential amendments etc., Minor and consequential amendments and repeals, Commencement, Extent & Short title

799.   These sections deal with the financial provision (section 275), commencement (section 279), territorial extent (section 280) and short title of the Act (section 281). Section 277 gives the Secretary of State power to make by order supplementary, incidental or consequential provision for the purposes of, or in consequence of, or for giving full effect to, the Act. Section 276 gives the Secretary of State power to introduce by order transitional or transitory provisions and savings as appropriate in connection with the coming into force of any provision in the Act. Schedule 24 sets out those transitional provisions that have already been identified, including the arrangements that will govern the handling of cases during the transition from the old FTA 1973 merger and monopoly regimes to their successor regimes. Section 278 gives effect to Schedules 25 and 26, which contain minor and consequential amendments, repeals and revocations.

COMMENCEMENT DATES

800.   All substantive provisions of the Act are to come into force by commencement orders.

HANSARD REFERENCES

801.   The following table sets out the dates and Hansard references for each stage of this Act's passage through Parliament.

Stage	Date	Hansard reference
House of Commons		
Introduction	26 March 2002	Vol 382 Col 703
Second Reading	10 April 2002	Vol 383 Cols 44-120
Committee	16, 18, 23, 25 and 30 April 2002; 1, 7, 9, 14 and 16 May 2002	Hansard Standing Committee B
Report and Third Reading	13 June 2002 and 17 June 2002	Vol 386 Cols 1033-1109 and Vol 387 Cols 22-125
House of Lords		
Introduction	19 June 2002	Vol 636 Col 741
Second Reading	2 July 2002	Vol 637 Cols 138-190

Committee	16, 18, 22, 29 and 30 July 2002	Vol 637 Cols 1095-1101, 1119-1166, 1187-1222; Vol 637 Cols 1427-1467, 1488-1544; Vol 638 Cols 132-180; Vol 638 Cols 738-745, 763-806; Vol 638 Cols 821-852
Report	15 and 21 October 2002	Vol 639 Cols 702-18, 732-3, 782-847; Vol 639 Cols 1070-1086, 1098-1143, 1160-1210
Third Reading	28 October 2002	Vol 640 Cols 12-18, 34-86

Royal Assent – 7 November 2002   House of Lords Hansard   Vol 640 Col 963
House of Commons Hansard Vol 392 Col 480

These notes refer to the Enterprise Act 2002 (c.40) which received Royal Assent on 7 November 2002

ANNEX A:
Path of a typical merger investigation in competition-only cases (i.e. where no intervention notice is served)

Main exceptions:
- OFT believe relevant customer benefits (CBs) outweigh SLC effect
- OFT seeks and obtains satisfactory undertaking(s) in lieu
- OFT believe market not of sufficient importance

STAGE 1: OFT

Timetable-
Merger notices: 20 days to refer (unless extensions apply)

Effective notice of completed merger: 4 months to refer (unless extensions apply)

OFT becomes aware of a merger (from: Merger notice, notice or material facts/publicity about a merger or otherwise)

↓

OFT assess whether it believes the merger qualifies for investigation, i.e.
- meets definition of a merger and
- meets share of supply test or turnover test

→ No → CLEAR

↓ Yes

OFT decides whether it believes merger may result in a substantial lessening of competition

→ No → CLEAR

↓ Yes

OFT has duty to refer to CC unless exceptions apply

STAGE 2: CC

Max. of 24 weeks to complete investigation (+ 8 weeks max. for special reasons) and report

CC decides whether
- a relevant merger situation has been created and
- the merger is expected to result in an SLC

→ No → CLEAR

↓

CC decide what action if any to take to remedy the SLC or adverse effects of the SLC. May have regard to customer benefits (CBs)

→ No action

↓

CC secures remedies by
- Seeking undertakings (which OFT may secure on its behalf)
- Making a final order

These notes refer to the Enterprise Act 2002 (c.40) which received Royal Assent on 7 November 2002

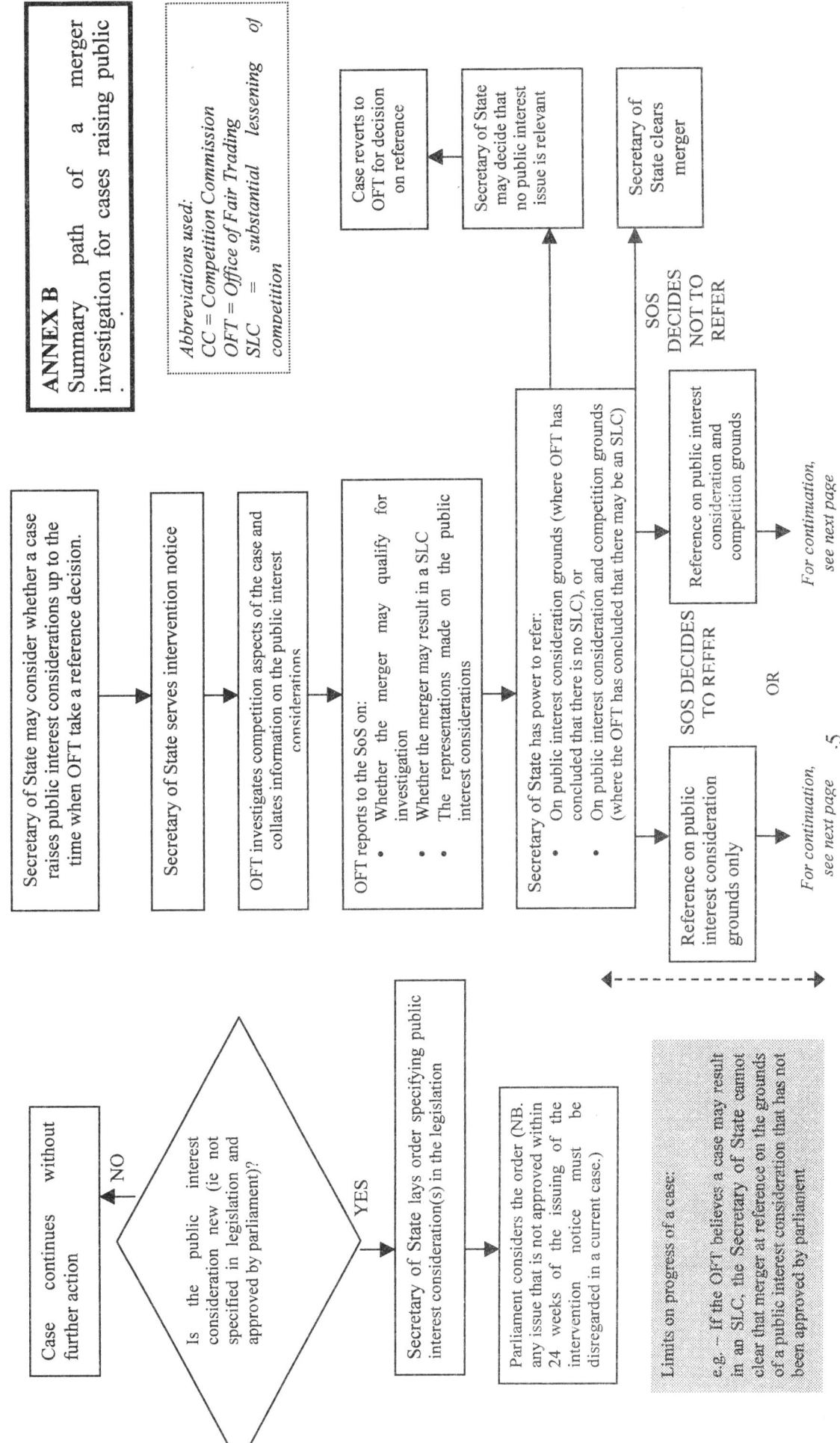

ANNEX B
Summary path of a merger investigation for cases raising public interest

Abbreviations used:
CC = Competition Commission
OFT = Office of Fair Trading
SLC = substantial lessening of competition

Secretary of State may consider whether a case raises public interest considerations up to the time when OFT take a reference decision.

Secretary of State serves intervention notice

OFT investigates competition aspects of the case and collates information on the public interest considerations

OFT reports to the SoS on:
• Whether the merger may qualify for investigation
• Whether the merger may result in a SLC
• The representations made on the public interest considerations

Secretary of State has power to refer:
• On public interest consideration grounds (where OFT has concluded that there is no SLC), or
• On public interest consideration and competition grounds (where the OFT has concluded that there may be an SLC)

SOS DECIDES TO REFER

Reference on public interest consideration grounds only

For continuation, see next page

SOS DECIDES NOT TO REFER

Reference on public interest consideration and competition grounds

For continuation, see next page

Case reverts to OFT for decision on reference

Secretary of State may decide that no public interest issue is relevant

Secretary of State clears merger

Case continues without further action

NO

Is the public interest consideration new (ie not specified in legislation and approved by parliament)?

YES

Secretary of State lays order specifying public interest consideration(s) in the legislation

Parliament considers the order (NB. any issue that is not approved within 24 weeks of the issuing of the intervention notice must be disregarded in a current case.)

Limits on progress of a case:

e.g. – If the OFT believes a case may result in an SLC, the Secretary of State cannot clear that merger at reference on the grounds of a public interest consideration that has not been approved by parliament

.5

*These notes refer to the Enterprise Act 2002 (c.40)
which received Royal Assent on 7 November 2002*

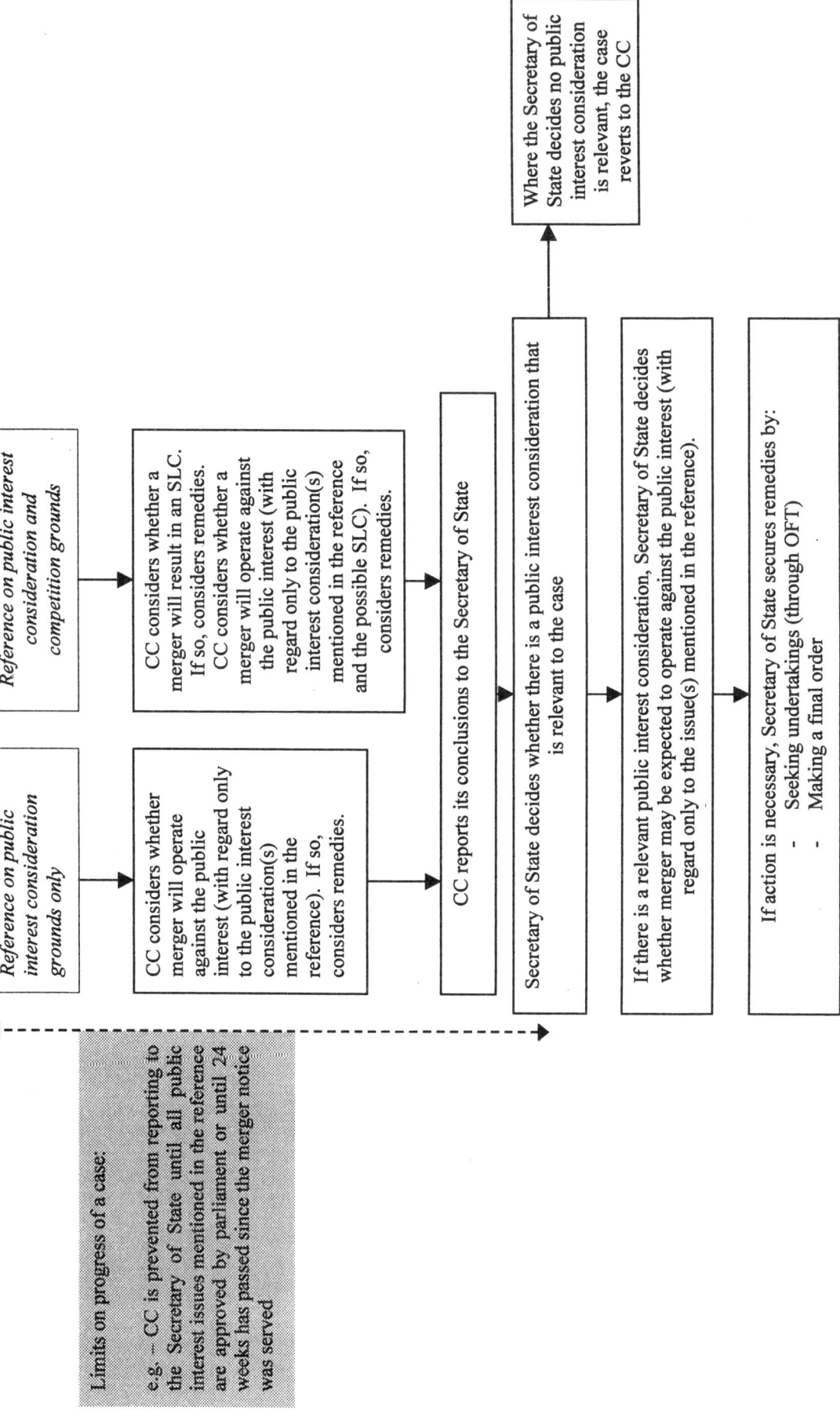

ANNEX C: MARKET PUBLIC INTEREST CASES

(a) Market Investigations

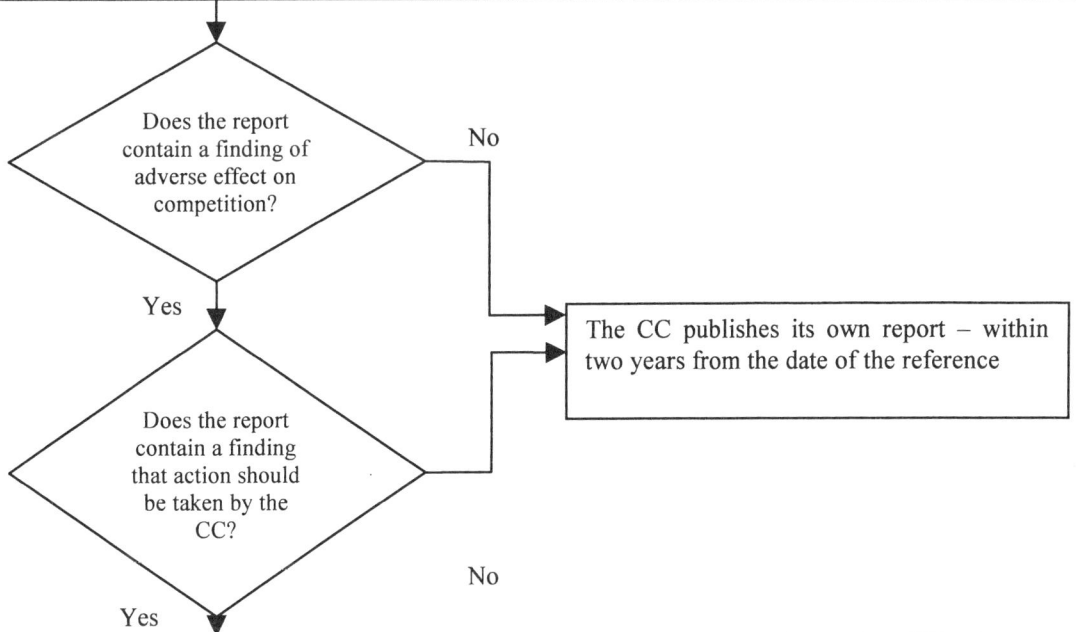

The Competition Commission is investigating a market investigation reference and no more than four months has passed since the date of the reference

Secretary of State believes that one or more public interest consideration may be relevant to the case

---

Secretary of State may serve an intervention notice

(Secretary of State may revoke an intervention notice at any time)

Competition Commission investigates and decides*:
- Whether there is an adverse effect on competition
- And, if so:
  - what action should be taken by the Secretary of State in light of the relevant public interest considerations, and what action could be taken by other persons to remedy the adverse effect on competition
  - what action should be taken and what is to be remedied if there were no relevant public interest considerations

---

Commission prepares report including its findings, reasons for those findings and further information for facilitating a proper understanding of the issues

---

Does the report contain a finding of adverse effect on competition?

No → The CC publishes its own report – within two years from the date of the reference

Yes

Does the report contain a finding that action should be taken by the CC?

No → The CC publishes its own report – within two years from the date of the reference

Yes

CC gives report to the Secretary of State – within two years from the date of the reference

CC will delay giving report to Secretary of State until 24 weeks after the intervention notice if there are non-finalised public interest considerations

CC will disregard public interest considerations that are not finalised on the giving of its report or within 24 weeks of the intervention notice

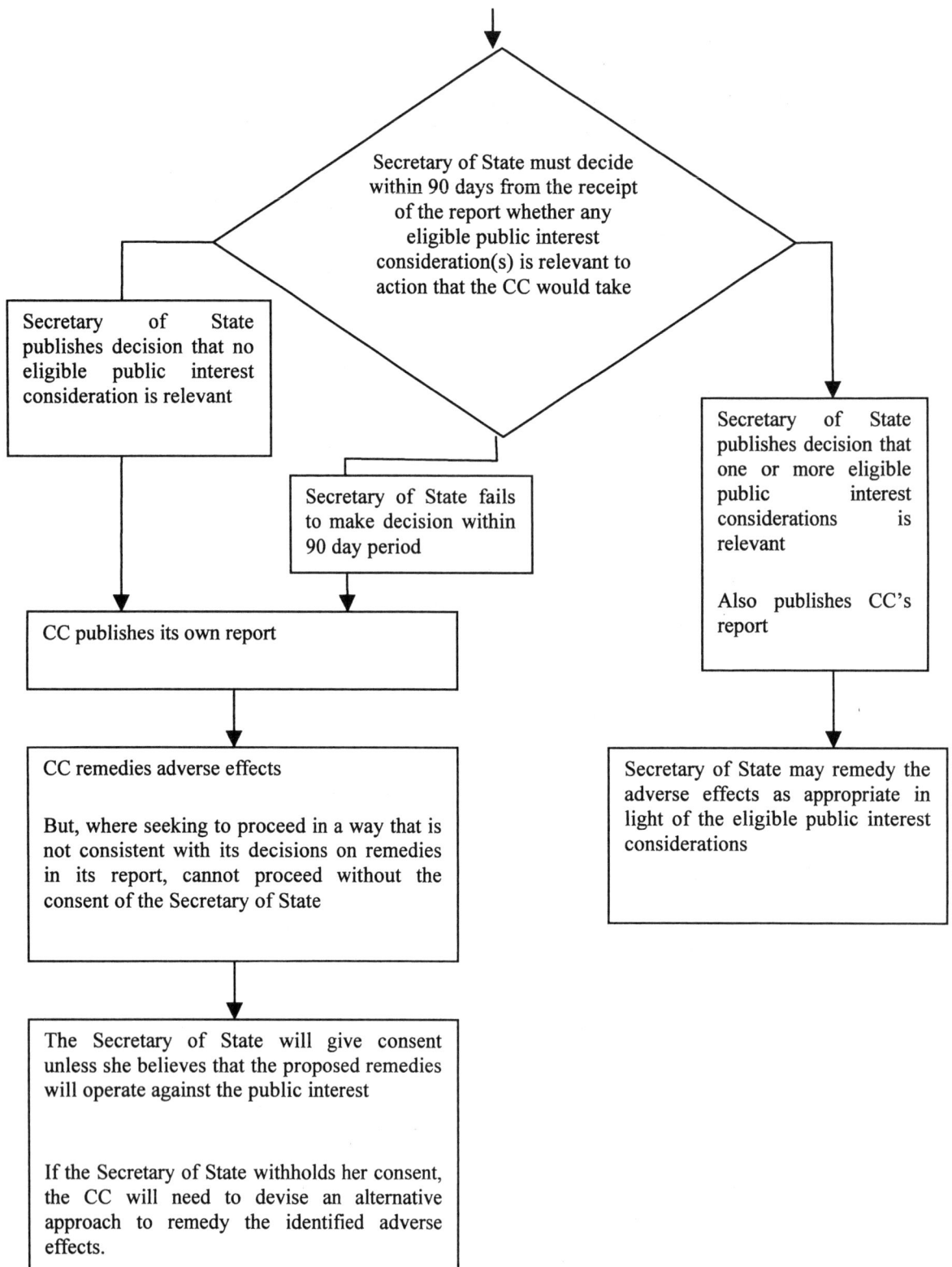

NOTE:

*Where an intervention notice is revoked or the Commission terminates its investigation because no relevant public interest considerations are finalised, the case will revert to the competition only route.

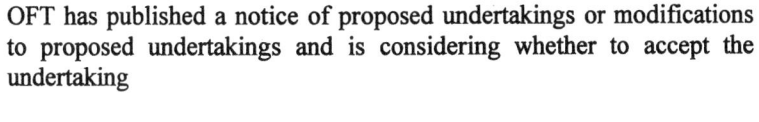

(b) Undertakings in Lieu

OFT has published a notice of proposed undertakings or modifications to proposed undertakings and is considering whether to accept the undertaking

Secretary of State believes that one or more public interest consideration may be relevant to the case

Secretary of State may serve an intervention notice any time before the undertaking is accepted

(Secretary of State may revoke an intervention notice at any time)

OFT prevented from accepting undertaking without the consent of the Secretary of State

Secretary of State will give consent unless:

Believes the undertaking will operate against the public interest

A public interest consideration mentioned in the intervention notice is not finalised and the intervention notice was served less than 24 weeks ago

OFT may accept the undertaking if consent is given.

Alternatively, (whether or not consent is given) the OFT may seek alternative undertakings or make a reference.

ANNEX D: MARKET INVESTIGATIONS: REMEDIES IN REGULATED MARKETS

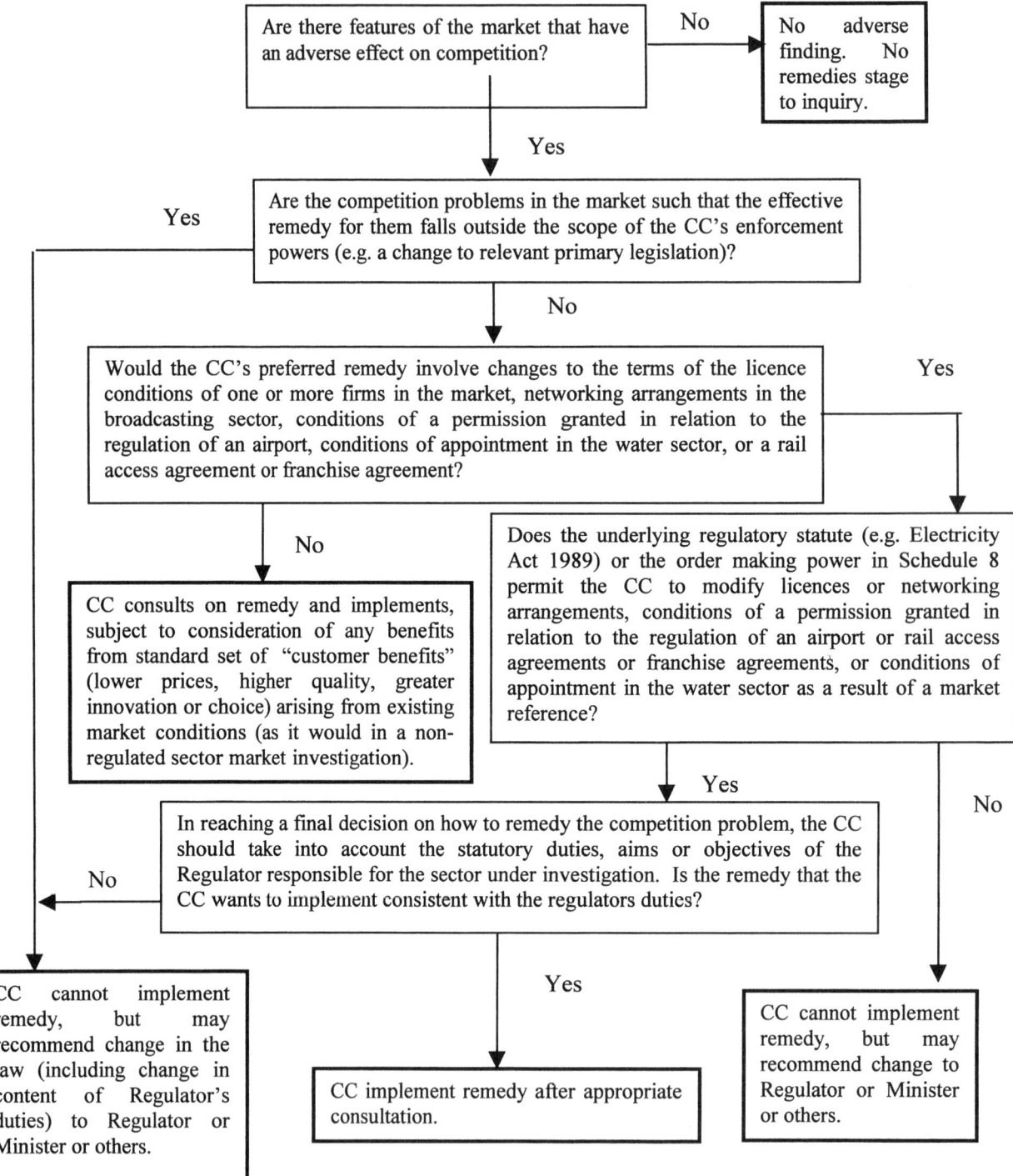

ANNEX E

Table of Correspondence	
Section in IA 86	**Paragraph in Schedule B1**
8(1)	11
8(2)	10
8(4)	8 and 9
9(1)	12(1)
9(2)(a)	12(2)
9(2)(b)	12(3)
9(3)	39
9(4)	13(1)
9(5)	13(3)
10	44
11(1)	40 and 41(1)
11(2)	41(2)
11(3)	42 and 43
11(4)	41(3)(a)
11(5)	41(3)(b)
12	45
13	10, 90 and 91
14(1)	59(1) and (2)
14(2)(a)	61
14(2)(b)	62
14(3)	63
14(4)	64
14(5)	69
14(6)	59(3)
15	70, 71 and 72
17(1)	67
17(2)	68
17(3)	56
18	79
19(1)	87 and 88
19(2)	89
19(4)-(10)	99(3)-(6)
20	98
24(1)	53(1)(a)
24(2)	53(1)(b)
24(4)	53(2)
24(5)	55
24(6) and (7)	86
25	54
26	57
27	74
27(6)	86
212	75
230(1)	6
231	100-103
232	104

ANNEX F

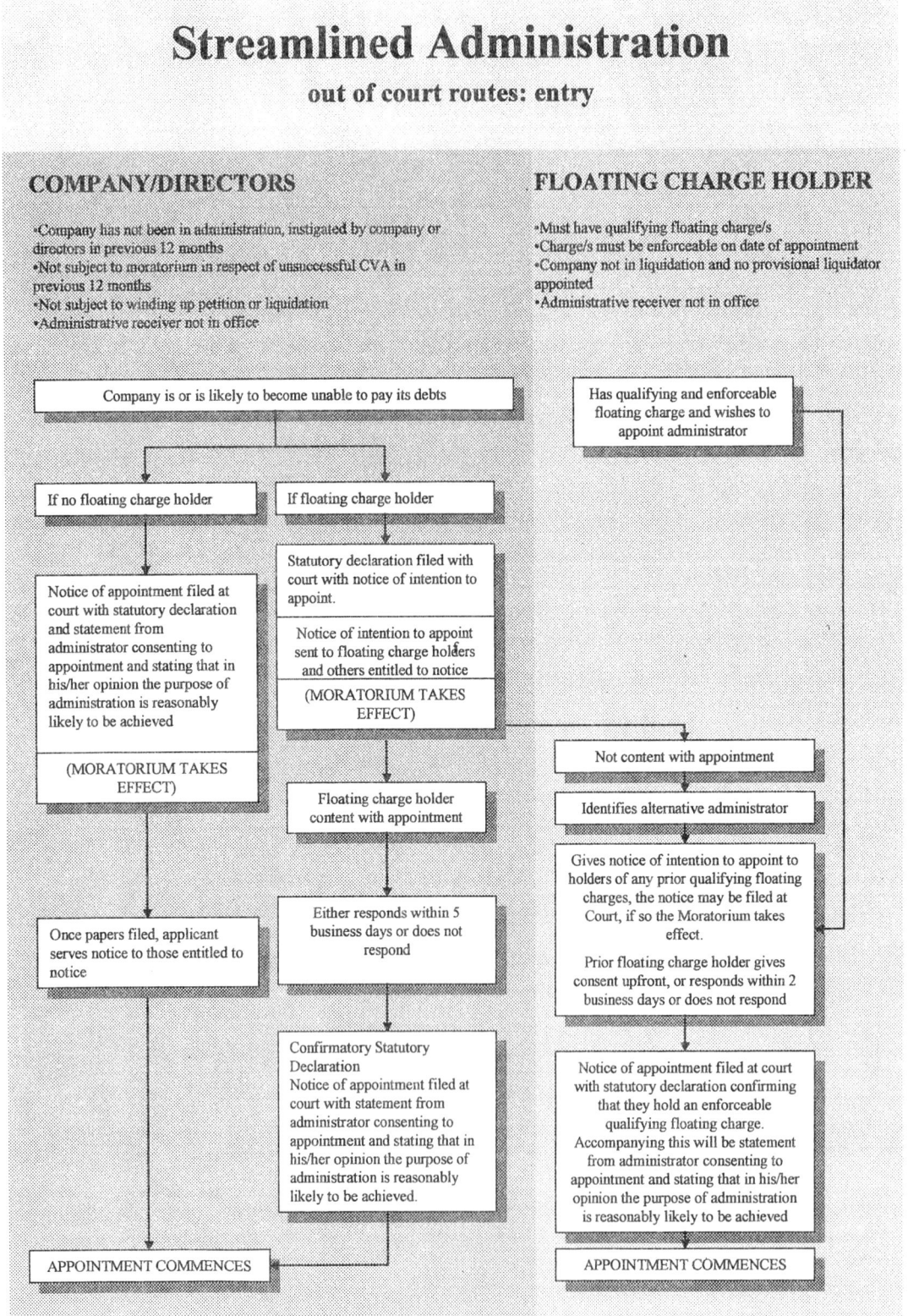

Streamlined Administration

out of court routes: entry

COMPANY/DIRECTORS

- Company has not been in administration, instigated by company or directors in previous 12 months
- Not subject to moratorium in respect of unsuccessful CVA in previous 12 months
- Not subject to winding up petition or liquidation
- Administrative receiver not in office

FLOATING CHARGE HOLDER

- Must have qualifying floating charge/s
- Charge/s must be enforceable on date of appointment
- Company not in liquidation and no provisional liquidator appointed
- Administrative receiver not in office

Company is or is likely to become unable to pay its debts

If no floating charge holder

If floating charge holder

Notice of appointment filed at court with statutory declaration and statement from administrator consenting to appointment and stating that in his/her opinion the purpose of administration is reasonably likely to be achieved

(MORATORIUM TAKES EFFECT)

Statutory declaration filed with court with notice of intention to appoint.

Notice of intention to appoint sent to floating charge holders and others entitled to notice

(MORATORIUM TAKES EFFECT)

Floating charge holder content with appointment

Once papers filed, applicant serves notice to those entitled to notice

Either responds within 5 business days or does not respond

Confirmatory Statutory Declaration
Notice of appointment filed at court with statement from administrator consenting to appointment and stating that in his/her opinion the purpose of administration is reasonably likely to be achieved.

APPOINTMENT COMMENCES

Has qualifying and enforceable floating charge and wishes to appoint administrator

Not content with appointment

Identifies alternative administrator

Gives notice of intention to appoint to holders of any prior qualifying floating charges, the notice may be filed at Court, if so the Moratorium takes effect.

Prior floating charge holder gives consent upfront, or responds within 2 business days or does not respond

Notice of appointment filed at court with statutory declaration confirming that they hold an enforceable qualifying floating charge. Accompanying this will be statement from administrator consenting to appointment and stating that in his/her opinion the purpose of administration is reasonably likely to be achieved

APPOINTMENT COMMENCES

ANNEX G

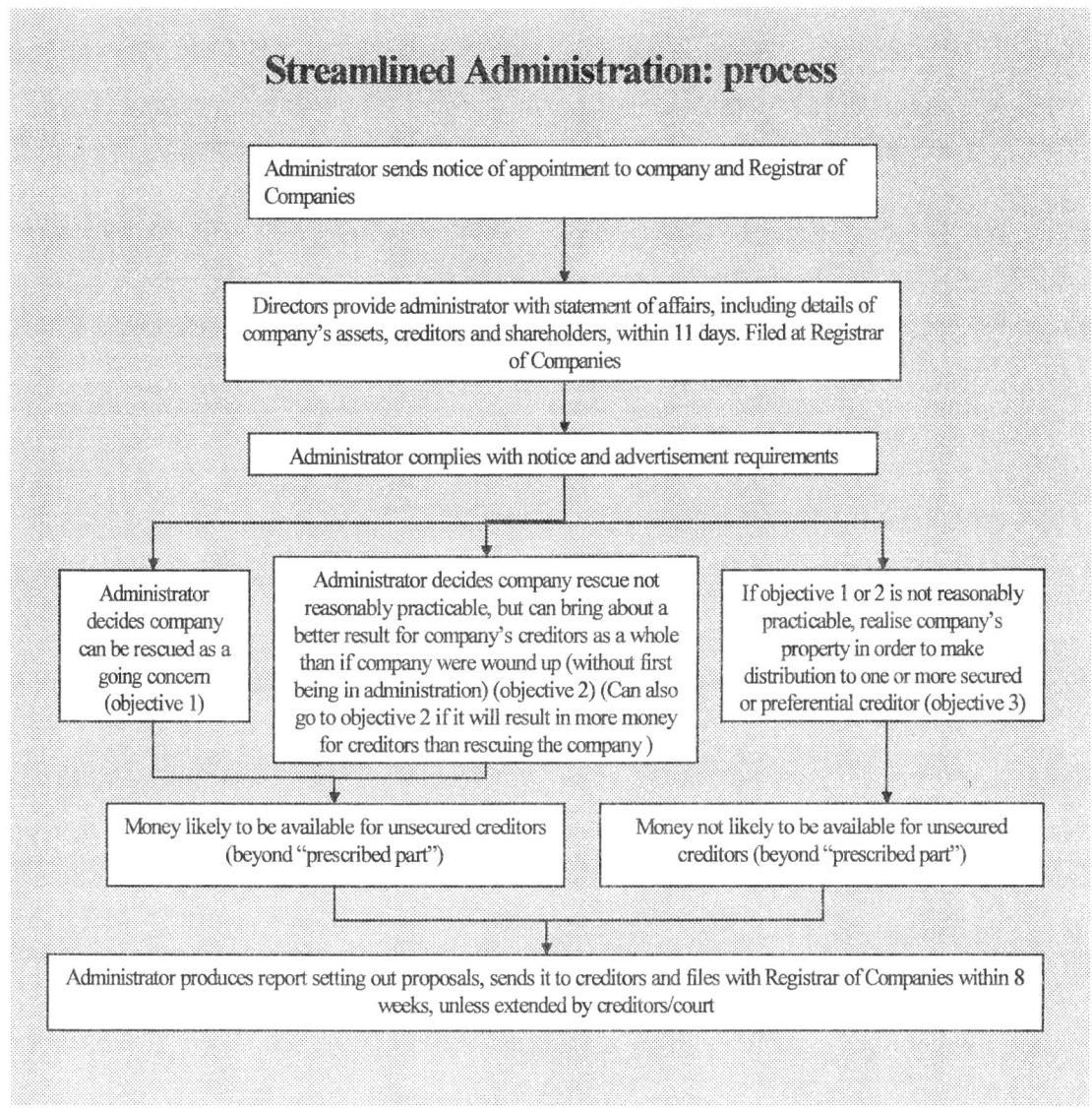

Streamlined Administration: process

Administrator sends notice of appointment to company and Registrar of Companies

Directors provide administrator with statement of affairs, including details of company's assets, creditors and shareholders, within 11 days. Filed at Registrar of Companies

Administrator complies with notice and advertisement requirements

Administrator decides company can be rescued as a going concern (objective 1)

Administrator decides company rescue not reasonably practicable, but can bring about a better result for company's creditors as a whole than if company were wound up (without first being in administration) (objective 2) (Can also go to objective 2 if it will result in more money for creditors than rescuing the company)

If objective 1 or 2 is not reasonably practicable, realise company's property in order to make distribution to one or more secured or preferential creditor (objective 3)

Money likely to be available for unsecured creditors (beyond "prescribed part")

Money not likely to be available for unsecured creditors (beyond "prescribed part")

Administrator produces report setting out proposals, sends it to creditors and files with Registrar of Companies within 8 weeks, unless extended by creditors/court

ANNEX H

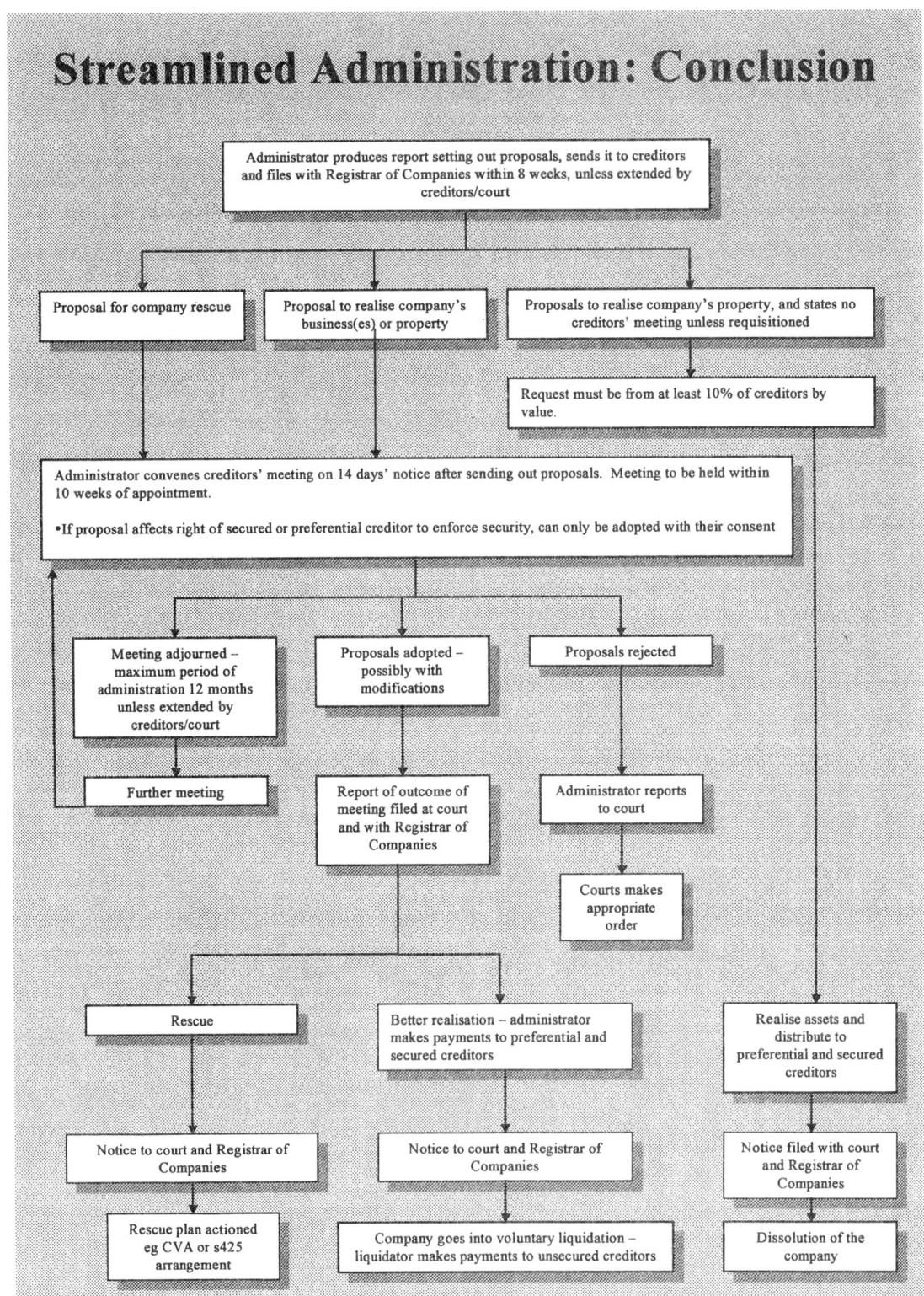

Streamlined Administration: Conclusion

Administrator produces report setting out proposals, sends it to creditors and files with Registrar of Companies within 8 weeks, unless extended by creditors/court

- Proposal for company rescue
- Proposal to realise company's business(es) or property
- Proposals to realise company's property, and states no creditors' meeting unless requisitioned

Request must be from at least 10% of creditors by value.

Administrator convenes creditors' meeting on 14 days' notice after sending out proposals. Meeting to be held within 10 weeks of appointment.

• If proposal affects right of secured or preferential creditor to enforce security, can only be adopted with their consent

- Meeting adjourned – maximum period of administration 12 months unless extended by creditors/court
- Proposals adopted – possibly with modifications
- Proposals rejected

- Further meeting
- Report of outcome of meeting filed at court and with Registrar of Companies
- Administrator reports to court

Courts makes appropriate order

- Rescue
- Better realisation – administrator makes payments to preferential and secured creditors
- Realise assets and distribute to preferential and secured creditors

- Notice to court and Registrar of Companies
- Notice to court and Registrar of Companies
- Notice filed with court and Registrar of Companies

- Rescue plan actioned eg CVA or s425 arrangement
- Company goes into voluntary liquidation – liquidator makes payments to unsecured creditors
- Dissolution of the company

Printed in the UK by The Stationery Office Limited
under the authority and superintendence of Carol Tullo, Controller of
Her Majesty's Stationery Office and Queen's Printer of Acts of Parliament